AL-MURSHID AL-MU'EEN
The Concise Guide to the Basics of the Deen

اَلْمُرْشِدُ الْمُعِينُ

عَلَى الضَّرُورِيِّ مِن عُلُومِ الدِّينِ

Al-Murshid al-Mu'een

THE CONCISE GUIDE TO
THE BASICS OF THE DEEN

ABD AL-WAHID IBN 'ASHIR

DIWAN PRESS

Classical and Contemporary Books on Islam and Sufism

Al-Murshid al-Mu'een

Published by: Diwan Press Ltd.
                   311 Allerton Road
                   Bradford
                   BD15 7HA
                   UK
Website: www.diwanpress.com
E-mail: info@diwanpress.com

By: Abu Muhammad Abd al-Wahid ibn 'Ashir
Translated by: Dr. Asadullah Yate
Typeset by: Abdassamad Clarke

A catalogue record of this book is available from the British Library.

ISBN-13:   978-1-908892-50-8 (Paperback)

CONTENTS

بسم الله الرحمن الرحيم

و الصلاة و السلام على سيدنا محمد

و على اله و صحبه اجمعين

١
يَقُولُ عَبْدُ الْوَاحِدِ بْنُ عَاشِر
مُبْتَدِئاً بِاسْمِ الْإِلَهِ الْقَادِرِ

1 Abd al-Wahid ibn 'Ashir says, beginning with the name of the Powerful God

٢
أَحْمَدُ لِلَّهِ الَّذِي عَلَّمَنَا
مِنَ الْعُلُومِ مَا بِهِ كَلَّفَنَا

2 Praise belongs to Allah Who has taught us the sciences which He has made incumbent upon us

٣
صَلَّى وَسَلَّمَ عَلَى مُحَمَّدٍ
وَآلِهِ وَصَحْبِهِ وَالْمُقْتَدِي

3 Then blessings and peace on Muhammad, his Family, Companions and those who follow his example

$$4 \qquad \text{وَبَعْدُ فَالْعَوْنُ مِنَ اللَّهِ الْمَجِيدْ}$$

$$\text{فِي نَظْمِ أَبْيَاتِ لِلْأُمِّيّ تُفِيدْ}$$

4   And then, help is from Allah, the Glorious, in the composition of verses which will be of benefit to the unlettered person…

$$5 \qquad \text{فِي عَقْدِ الْأَشْعَرِي وفِقْهِ مَالِكْ}$$

$$\text{وَفِي طَرِيقَةِ الْجُنَيْدِ السَّالِكْ}$$

5   on the subject of the 'aqida of al-Ash'ari, the fiqh of Malik and the tariqa of al-Junaid, the wayfarer.

مُقَدِّمَةٌ لِكِتَابِ الْاعْتِقَادِ

مُعِينَةٌ لِقَارِئِهَا عَلَى الْمُرَادِ

INTRODUCTION
TO THE BOOK OF 'AQIDA

WHICH IS AN AID TO ACTS OF OBEDIENCE
AND ATTAINING THE DESIRED GOAL

وَحُكْمُنَا الْعَقْلِي قَضِيَّةٌ بِلَا

6

وَقْفٍ عَلَى عَادَةٍ أَوْ وَضْعٍ جَلَا

6   Our (pure) intellectual judgement is a proposition
     which is independent of anything learned by
     repeated experience or from customary usage
     which is clear (from the shari'ah).

أَقْسَامُ مُقْتَضَاهُ بِالْحَصْرِ تُمَازْ

7

وَهِيَ الْوُجُوبُ الِاسْتِحَالَةُ الْجَوَازْ

7   The requisite divisions encompassing the judgement
     as a whole are differentiated into the necessarily
     true, the inconceivable and the conceivable

$$\text{فَوَاجِبٌ لَا يَقْبَلُ النَّفْيَ بِحَالْ} \qquad 8$$
$$\text{ومَا أَبَى الثُّبُوتَ عَقْلاً الْمُحَالْ}$$

8   The 'necessarily true' refers to that which does not admit of negation whatsoever, and that which the intellect refuses to attest to is the 'inconceivable'.

$$\text{وجَائِزاً مَاقَبِلَ الْأَمْرَيْنِ سِمْ} \qquad 9$$
$$\text{لِلضَّرُورِي والنَّظَرِي كُلٌّ قُسِمْ}$$

9   'Conceivable' is a term applied to that which admits of the two (aforementioned) terms, and the description *daruri* (i.e. a necessary judgement immediately apparent to all) or *nadhari* (a judgement only apparent upon reflection) may be (further) applied to each of the (three) divisions.

$$\text{أَوَّلُ وَاجِبٍ عَلَى مَنْ كُلِّفَا} \qquad 10$$
$$\text{مُمَكَّناً مِنْ نَظَرٍ أَنْ يَعْرِفَا}$$

10   The first thing which is incumbent upon the legally capable person – as long as he is capable of reflection – is that he know...

$$\text{اللَّهَ وَالرُّسُلَ بِالصِّفَاتِ}$$

$$\text{مِمَّا عَلَيْهِ نَصَبَ الآيَاتِ}$$

11 Allah and the Messengers by the attributes and qualities set out in the ayats

$$\text{وَكُلُّ تَكْلِيفٍ بِشَرْطِ الْعَقْلِ}$$

$$\text{مَعَ الْبُلُوغِ بِدَمٍ أَوْ حَمْلِ}$$

12 Every imposition of a duty is conditional upon the person being of sane mind, having reached puberty – recognised by the onset of menstruation or pregnancy, (in the case of young women)

$$\text{أَوْ بِمَنِيٍّ أَوْ بِإِنْبَاتِ الشَّعَرِ}$$

$$\text{أَوْ بِثَمَانِ عَشْرَةٍ حَوْلاً ظَهَرْ}$$

13 Or by the presence of sperm, or the growth of (pubic) hair or (in the absence of any of these signs), the completion of eighteen years.

كِتَابُ أُمِّ الْقَوَاعِدِ

وَمَا انْطَوَتْ عَلَيْهِ مِنَ الْعَقَائِدِ

THE BOOK OF BASIC PRINCIPLES
REGARDING 'AQIDA

يَجِبُ لِلَّهِ الْوُجُودُ وَالْقِدَمْ   14

كَذَا الْبَقَاءُ وَالْغِنَى الْمُطْلَقُ عَمْ

14   It is necessarily true that Allah have existence and
that this existence is from before endless time,
and likewise that He possess going on, and
absolute independence universally

وَخُلْفُهُ لِخَلْقِهِ بِلَا مِثَالْ   15

وَوَحْدَةُ الذَّاتِ وَوَصْفٍ وَالْفِعَالْ

15   And His being different from His creation without
resemblance, and His Oneness of essence, of
attribute and action

$$\text{وَقُدْرَةٌ إِرَادَةٌ عِلْمٌ حَيَاةْ}$$
$$\text{سَمْعٌ كَلَامٌ بَصَرٌ ذِي وَاجِبَاتْ}$$

16 And power, will, knowledge, life, hearing, speech, sight; these are necessarily true (for Him)

$$\text{وَيَسْتَحِيلُ ضِدُّ هَذِهِ الصِّفَاتْ}$$
$$\text{الْعَدَمُ الْحُدُوثُ ذَا لِلْحَادِثَاتِ}$$

17 And the opposite of these attributes are inconceivable (for Him – like) non-existence, coming into being in time (*al-hudouth*); that is for originated things.

$$\text{كَذَا الْفَنَا وَالِافْتِقَارُ عُدَّهْ}$$
$$\text{وَأَنْ يُمَاثَلَ وَنَفْيُ الْوِحْدَةْ}$$

18 Likewise, annihilation, being in need of other than Him, count them! And He be like (anything else) or His oneness be negated,

$$\text{عَجْزٌ كَرَاهَةٌ وَجَهْلٌ وَمَمَاتْ}$$
$$\text{وَصَمَمٌ وَبَكَمٌ عَمًى صُمَاتْ}$$

19 Incapacity, unwillingness, ignorance, death, deafness, dumbness, blindness or silence

$$\text{يَجُوزُ فِي حَقِّهِ فِعْلُ الْمُمْكِنَاتْ}$$
$$\text{بِأَسْرِهَا وَتَرْكُهَا فِي الْعَدَمَاتْ}$$

20

20 It is conceivable with respect to Him that He carry out anything that is possible or leave (all) that is possible in (a state of) non-existence.

$$\text{الدَّلَائِلُ}$$

THE EVIDENCES

$$\text{وُجُودُهُ لَهُ دَلِيلٌ قَاطِعْ}$$
$$\text{حَاجَةُ كُلِّ مُحْدَثٍ لِلصَّانِعْ}$$

21

21 His existence has an absolute proof: every in-time, creational occurrence needs a Creator

$$\text{لَوْ حَدَثَتْ بِنَفْسِهَا الْأَكْوَانُ}$$
$$\text{لَا جْتَمَعَ التَّسَاوِي وَالرُّجْحَانُ}$$

22

22 If beings had originated of themselves, then the equal probability (of existence and non-existence) and the (fact of) the preponderance (of existence, in that beings do exist) would be united –

$$\text{وَذَا مُحَالٌ وَحُدُوثُ الْعَالَمِ} \qquad 23$$

$$\text{مِنْ حَدَثِ الأَعْرَاضِ مَعْ تَلَازُمِ}$$

23 and this is inconceivable, and the coming into existence of the world is necessarily a coming into being of contingent, incidental occurrence.

$$\text{لَوْ لَمْ يَكُ الْقِدَمُ وَصْفَهُ لَزِمْ} \qquad 24$$

$$\text{حُدُوثُهُ دَوْرٌ تَسَلْسُلٌ حُتِمْ}$$

24 If His attribute were not timelessness then His coming into being in time as a chain of events would be necessarily true

$$\text{لَوْ أَمْكَنَ الْفَنَاءُ لَاتَنَفَى الْقِدَمْ} \qquad 25$$

$$\text{لَوْ مَاثَلَ الْخَلْقَ حُدُوثُهُ الْحُتِمْ}$$

25 If annihilation were possible, then timelessness would be nullified. If He resembled creation, His coming-into-being would be necessarily true

$$\text{لَوْ لَمْ يَجِبْ وَصْفُ الْغِنَى لَهُ افْتَقَرْ} \qquad 26$$

$$\text{لَوْ لَمْ يَكُنْ بِوَاحِدٍ لَمَا قَدَرْ}$$

26 If the attribute of independence were not necessarily true (with respect to Him) He would be in need; if He were not One, He would have no power.

لَوْ لَمْ يَكُنْ حَيّاً مُرِيداً عَالِماً ٢٧

وَقَادِراً لَمَا رَأَيْتَ عَالَمَا

27 If He were not Living, Willing, Knowing, and Powerful you would not see the universe –

وَالتَّالِ فِي السِّتِّ الْقَضَايَا بَاطِلْ ٢٨

قَطْعاً مُقَدَّمٌ إِذاً مُمَاثِلْ

28 Any consequence of these six (propositions) is absolutely false; thus any preceding (premise) is likewise false

وَالسَّمْعُ وَالْبَصَرُ وَالْكَلَامْ ٢٩

بِالنَّقْلِ مَعْ كَمَالِهِ تُرَامْ

29 and (proof of His) hearing, seeing, and speech (is afforded) by transmission – and also (by deduction from) His perfection

لَوْ اِسْتَحَالَ مُمْكِنٌ أَوْ وَجَبَا ٣٠

قَلْبُ الْحَقَائِقِ لُزُوماً أَوْجَبَا

30 If the conceivable became inconceivable or necessarily true, realities and truths would necessarily be turned upside down.

$$\text{يَجِبُ لِلرُّسْلِ الْكِرَامِ الصِّدْقُ}$$
$$\text{أَمَانَةٌ تَبْلِيغُهُمْ يَحِقُّ}$$

31

31 It is necessarily true that the noble Messengers are truthful, trustworthy and convey all of the message.

$$\text{مُحَالُ الْكَذِبُ وَالْمَنْهِيُّ}$$
$$\text{كَعَدَمِ التَّبْلِيغِ يَا ذَكِيُّ}$$

32

32 Impossible are lying, and what is forbidden, as well as not conveying the Message, O man of intellect!

$$\text{يَجُوزُ فِي حَقِّهِمْ كُلُّ عَرَضْ}$$
$$\text{لَيْسَ مُؤَدِّياً لِنَقْصٍ كَالْمَرَضْ}$$

33

33 Every (human) contingency is conceivable with respect to them, like illness, as long as this does not imply any imperfection

$$\text{لَوْ لَمْ يَكُونُوا صَادِقِينَ لَزِمْ}$$
$$\text{أَنْ يَكْذِبَ الْإِلَهُ فِي تَصْدِيقِهِمْ}$$

34

34 If they were not truthful, it would be necessarily follow that God had told a lie in confirming them
—

$$\text{إِذْ مُعْجِزَاتُهُمْ كَقَوْلِهِ وَبَرّْ}$$

$$\text{صَدَقَ هَذَا الْعَبْدُ فِي كُلِّ خَبَرْ}$$

35

35 Since their miracles are equivalent to His saying: 'He is truthful! This slave has spoken the truth in everything he reports'

$$\text{لَوِ انْتَفَى التَّبْلِيغُ أَوْ خَانُوا حُتِمْ}$$

$$\text{أَنْ يُقْلَبَ الْمَنْهِيُّ طَاعَةً لَهُمْ}$$

36

36 If the conveyance of the Message (by the Messengers) went unfulfilled or they were to betray the trust (Allah had placed in them), then (the judgement regarding) something forbidden (by Allah) would be reversed – by the act of obedience to their (disobedience).

$$\text{جَوَازُ الْأَغْرَاضِ عَلَيْهِمْ حُجَّتُهُ}$$

$$\text{وُقُوعُهَا بِهِمْ تَسَلٍّ حِكْمَتُهُ}$$

37

37 The proof that contingencies can happen to them is that they occurred (and were witnessed); their patient endurance (of whatever occurred) was by His wisdom.

$$\text{38} \quad \text{وَقَوْلُ لَا إِلَهَ إِلاَّ اللَّهُ}$$
$$\text{مُحَمَّدٌ أَرْسَلَهُ الْإِلَهُ}$$

38 The declarations 'there is no god except Allah and
    Muhammad has been sent by God',

$$\text{39} \quad \text{يَجْمَعُ كُلَّ هَذِهِ الْمَعَانِي}$$
$$\text{كَانَتْ لِذَا عَلَامَةَ الْإِيمَانِ}$$

39 Unites all these meanings and for this reason it is
    the indication of Iman

$$\text{40} \quad \text{وَهِيَ أَفْضَلُ وُجُوهِ الذِّكْرِ}$$
$$\text{فَاشْغَلْ بِهَا الْعُمْرَ تَفُزْ بِالذُّخْرِ}$$

40 And it is the best kind of dhikr, and so occupy your
    life with it and you will win a great treasure.

The Book of Basic Principles Regarding 'Aqida

فَصْلٌ فِي قَوَاعِدِ الْإِسْلَامِ

SECTION ON
THE PILLARS OF ISLAM

فَصْلٌ وَطَاعَةُ الْجَوَارِحِ الْجَمِيعْ 41
قَوْلاً وَفِعْلاً هُوَ الْإِسْلَامُ الرَّفِيعْ

41 Section: Obedience of all the limbs both in speech
and action – this is elevated Islam.

قَوَاعِدُ الْإِسْلَامِ خَمْسٌ وَاجِبَاتْ 42
وَهِيَ الشَّهَادَتَانِ شَرْطُ الْبَاقِيَاتْ

42 The pillars of Islam are five obligations, the first being
the two shahadas – which are prerequisite for the
rest,

ثُمَّ الصَّلاةُ والزَّكَاةُ فِي الْقِطَاعْ 43
والصَّوْمُ والْحَجُّ عَلَى مَنِ اسْتَطَاعْ

43 then the salat, the zakat – on what is zakatable, the
fasting and the hajj for the one who is able.

$$\text{الْإِيمَانُ جَزْمٌ بِالإِلَهِ وَالْكُتُبْ} \quad 44$$
$$\text{وَالرُّسْلِ وَالأَمْلَاكِ مَعْ بَعْثٍ قَرُبْ}$$

44 Iman is unwavering trust in Allah, the Books, the Messengers, the Angels, the imminent Raising up (of mankind),

$$\text{وَقَدَرٌ كَذَا الصِّرَاطُ فَالْمِيزَانْ} \quad 45$$
$$\text{حَوْضُ النَّبِيّ جَنَّةٌ وَنِيرَانْ}$$

45 the Decree, the Sirat-bridge, the Balance, the Fountain of the Prophet, the Garden and the Fire.

$$\text{وَأَمَّا الْإِحْسَانُ فَقَالَ مَنْ دَرَاهْ} \quad 46$$
$$\text{أَنْ تَعْبُدَ اللَّهَ كَأَنَّكَ تَرَاهْ}$$

46 As for Ihsan the one who knows said that you should 'worship Allah as if you can see Him'

$$\text{إِنْ لَمْ تَكُنْ تَرَاهُ إِنَّهُ يَرَاكْ} \quad 47$$
$$\text{وَالدِّينُ ذِي الثَّلَاثِ خُذْ أَقْوَى عُرَاكْ}$$

47 and that 'if you cannot see Him (then know that) He sees you.' The deen has three aspects – so take hold of the firmest of supports.

مُقَدِّمَةٌ مِنَ الْأُصُولِ

مُعِينَةٌ فِي فُرُوعِهَا عَلَى الْوُصُولِ

– FROM THE ROOTS –
WHOSE BRANCHES ARE AN AID TO ARRIVAL

اَلْحُكْمُ فِي الشَّرْعِ خِطَابُ رَبِّنَا ‎48

الْمُقْتَضِي فِعْلَ الْمُكَلَّفِ افْطَنَا

48 The judgement in the Law is that our Lord's addressing us requires action on behalf of the *mukallaf* – O take note of this! –

بِطَلَبٍ أَوْإِذْنٍ أَوْبِوَضْع ‎49

لِسَبَبٍ أَوْشَرْطٍ أَوْ ذِي مَنْع

49 action which is demanded, or permitted or set out by virtue of a reason, condition or prohibition.

أَقْسَامُ حُكْمِ الشَّرْعِ خَمْسَةٌ تُرَامْ 50

فَرْضٌ وَنَدْبٌ وَكَرَاهَةٌ حَرَامْ

50 The divisions of the judgements in the shari'a
are five: obligatory (*fard*), recommended (*nadb*),
disliked (*makruh*), prohibited (*haram*) and

ثُمَّ إِبَاحَةٌ فَمَأْمُورٌ جُزِمْ 51

فَرْضٌ وَدُونَ الْجَزْمِ مَنْدُوبٌ وُسِمْ

51 permitted (*ibaha*). An absolute command is
obligatory, and that which is other than absolute
is recommended, so take note!

ذُو النَّهْيِ مَكْرُوهٌ وَمَعْ حَتْمٍ حَرَامْ 52

مَأْذُونُ وَجْهَيْهِ مُبَاحٌ ذَا تَمَامْ

52 That which contains an interdiction (*nahy*)
is disliked, and when absolute, then it is a
prohibition, that which is permitted means one
is allowed (either to do it or not to do it) – and
this completes (the five).

وَالْفَرْضُ قِسْمَانِ كِفَايَةٌ وَعَيْنْ
وَيَشْمَلُ الْمَنْدُوبُ سُنَّةً بِذَيْنْ

53　The obligatory is of two types, the collective and
the individual and the 'recommended' (as a
general term) includes the (more specific term)
'sunna' with respect to both (the latter).

كِتَابُ الطَّهَارَةِ

THE BOOK OF PURIFICATION

54   فَصْلٌ وَتَحْصُلُ الطَّهَارَةُ بِمَا
مِنَ التَّغَيُّرِ بِشَيْءٍ سَلِمَا

54   Purification is obtained by means of water which
has not been adulterated by anything.

55   إِذَا تَغَيَّرَ بِنَجْسٍ طُرِحَا
أَوْ طَاهِرٍ لِعَادَةٍ قَدْ صَلُحَا

55   If it has been adulterated with something impure, it
is to be rejected; likewise (it is to be rejected), even
if pure – although it may be used for day to day
(non ritual) use -

56   إِلاَّ إِذَا لَازَمَهُ فِي الْغَالِبِ
كَمُغْرَةٍ فَمُطْلَقٌ كَالذَّائِبِ

56   unless this pure thing is usually part of the water,
like the red colouring (of turf) – in which case
it is deemed good for all purposes, and likewise
melted water (from snow).

فَرَائِضُ الْوُضُوءِ

THE OBLIGATIONS OF WUDU'

فَصْلٌ فَرَائِضُ الْوُضُوءِ سَبْعٌ وَهِيَ
دَلْكٌ وَفَوْرٌ نِيَّةٌ فِي بَدْئِهِ

57

57 Section: The obligations of the wudu' are seven in number and they are rubbing (the water over the skin), (performing the various acts of wudu') one after the other without interruption, and intention at the beginning.

وَلْيَنْوِ رَفْعَ حَدَثٍ أَوْ مُفْتَرَضْ
أَوِ اسْتِبَاحَةً لِمَمْنُوعٍ عَرَضْ

58

58 One then makes the intention to remove an impurity, to perform an obligation, or to make permissible what was forbidden

وَغَسْلُ وَجْهٍ غَسْلُهُ الْيَدَيْنِ
وَمَسْحُ رَأْسٍ غَسْلُهُ الرِّجْلَيْنِ

59

59 (then) washes one's face, one's hands and forearms, wipes one's head, and washes one's feet

$$\text{وَالْفَرْضُ عَمَّ مَجْمَعَ الْأُذُنَيْنِ}$$
$$\text{وَالْمِرْفَقَيْنِ عَمَّ وَالْكَعْبَيْنِ}$$

60

60 It is obligatory to cover up to the junction (– with the face –) of one's ears (when washing), and up to (and including) the elbows and the ankles.

$$\text{خَلِّلْ أَصَابِعَ الْيَدَيْنِ وَشَعَرْ}$$
$$\text{وَجْهٍ إِذَا مَا تَحْتَهُ الْجِلْدُ ظَهَرْ}$$

61

61 (and) to rub between the fingers and the hair of the face if the skin is visible beneath it.

$$\text{سُنَنُ الْوُضُوءِ}$$

THE SUNAN OF WUDU'

$$\text{سُنَنُهُ السَّبْعُ ابْتِدَا غَسْلُ الْيَدَيْنِ}$$
$$\text{وَرَدُّ مَسْحِ الرَّأْسِ مَسْحُ الْأُذُنَيْنِ}$$

62

62 The sunnas are seven in number: one begins by washing each hand, (then) one wipes one's head from the back (to the front) and ears

مَضْمَضَةُ اسْتِنْشَاقُ اسْتِنْثَارُ ۶۳

تَرْتِيبُ فَرْضِهِ وَذَا الْمُخْتَارُ

63 (then) one rinses one's mouth, sniffing up water into the nose, blowing out (and) performs the obligatory elements in order – this is the preferred (judgement).

وَأَحَدَ عَشْرَ الْفَضَائِلُ أَتَتْ ۶٤

تَسْمِيَةٌ وَبُقْعَةٌ قَدْ طَهُرَتْ

64 There are eleven praiseworthy aspects: saying bismillah, a clean place,

تَقْلِيلُ مَاءٍ وَتَيَامُنُ الْإِنَا ۶٥

وَالشَّفْعُ وَالتَّثْلِيثُ فِي مَغْسُولِنَا

65 using little water, placing the receptacle on the right, washing a second and third time,

بَدْءُ الْمَيَامِنِ سِوَاكُ وَنُدِبْ ۶۶

تَرْتِيبُ مَسْنُونِهِ أَوْ مَعَ مَا يَجِبْ

66 beginning with the right (side of one's body), (using the) miswak, (keeping to) the order of the sunnas and (within the order of) what is obligatory

وَبَدْءُ مَسْحِ الرَّأْسِ مِنْ مُقَدَّمِهْ

تَخْلِيلُهُ أَصَابِعاً بِقَدَمِهْ

67   and beginning with the wiping of the head from the
     front, and rubbing in water between the toes of the
     feet.

وَكُرِهَ الزَّيْدُ عَلَى الْفَرْضِ لَدَى

مَسْحٍ وَفِي الْغَسْلِ عَلَى مَا حُدِّدَا

68   It is disliked to do more than what is prescribed in
     the obligatory – when wiping and washing.

وَعَاجِزُ الْفَوْرِ بَنَى مَا لَمْ يَطُلْ

بِيُبْسِ الأَعْضَا فِي زَمَانٍ مُعْتَدِلْ

69   If one is unable to do each element of the wudu'
     consecutively, one should carry on where one left
     off, as long as the time which elapses is not so
     long that the limbs – in a moderate temperature
     – have dried.

70   ذَاكِرُ فَرْضِهِ بِطُولٍ يَفْعَلُهُ

فَقَطْ وَفِي الْقُرْبِ الْمُوَالِي يُكْمِلُهُ

70   The person who remembers an obligation after a
long time has elapsed should do just this; but after
a short time, he should complete with continuity;

71   إِنْ كَانَ صَلَّى بَطَلَتْ وَمَنْ ذَكَرْ

سُنَّتَهُ يَفْعَلُهَا لِمَا حَضَرْ

71   if he has (already) performed the salat, then the
(salat) is invalid, and whoever remembers one of
the sunnas should do it when he remembers.

نَوَاقِضُ الْوُضُوءِ

THAT WHICH BREAKS WUDU'

72   نَوَاقِضُ الْوُضُوء سِتَّةَ عَشَرْ

بَوْلٌ وَرِيحٌ سَلَسٌ إِذَا نَدَرْ

72   The things which break the wudu' are sixteen in
number: urinating, breaking wind, incontinence
if infrequent

$$73 \quad \text{وَغَائِطٌ نَوْمٌ ثَقِيلٌ مَذْيُ}$$
$$\text{سُكْرٌ وَإِغْمَاءٌ جُنُونٌ وَدْيُ}$$

73 and defecating, deep sleep, discharge of *madhi* (thin, pre-seminal fluid), intoxication, fainting, madness or discharge of (the thicker fluid) *wadyi* (discharged after urination),

$$74 \quad \text{لَمْسٌ وَقُبْلَةٌ وَذَا إِنْ وُجِدَتْ}$$
$$\text{لَذَّةُ عَادَةٍ كَذَا إِنْ قُصِدَتْ}$$

74 touching (a woman) and kissing if (sexual) pleasure is experienced, or if intended,

$$75 \quad \text{إِلْطَافُ مَرْأَةٍ كَذَا مَسُّ الذَّكَرْ}$$
$$\text{وَالشَّكُّ فِي الْحَدَثِ كُفْرُ مَنْ كَفَرْ}$$

75 a woman touching inside her vagina, a man touching his penis (with his palm), doubt as to whether one has become impure, and becoming a kafir.

وَيَجِبُ اسْتِبْرَاءُ الأَخْبَثَيْنِ مَعْ

سَلِّ وَنَتْرِ ذَكَرٍ وَالشَّدَّ دَعْ

76 It is obligatory to free the 'two places of filth' of the (last remains of) urine and excrement, and to apply pressure to the penis and shake it but not excessively.

وَجَازَ الاِسْتِجْمَارُ مِنْ بَوْلِ ذَكَرْ

كَغَائِطٍ لَا مَا كَثِيراً اِنْتَشَرْ

77

77 It is permitted to use (only) stones to clean urine from the penis, and to clean oneself of excrement (with them) – as long as it has not spread excessively (beyond the anus itself).

الْغُسْل

GHUSL

فَرَائِضُ الْغُسْل

OBLIGATIONS OF GHUSL

فَصْلٌ فُرُوضُ الغُسْلِ قَصْدٌ يُحْتَضَرْ
فَوْرٌ عُمُومُ الدَّلْكِ تَخْلِيلُ الشَّعَرْ

78

78   Section: the *fard* obligations of the ghusl are: that
one's intent be present, that one complete the
various elements of the ghusl one after each other
without interruption, one rub all over (the body)
and ensure that water penetrates the hair (to the
skin)

فَتَابِـع انْخَفِيَّ مِثْلَ الرُّكْبَتَيْنِ
وَالْإِبْطِ وَالرَّفْغِ وَبَيْنَ الْأَلْيَتَيْنِ

79

79   and see (that the water reaches) the recesses (of the
body) and folds (of the skin), like behind the knees
and the armpits, the junction of the thighs and
the buttocks

$$\text{وَصِلْ لِمَا عَسُرَ بِالْمِنْدِيلِ} \qquad 80$$
$$\text{وَنَحْوِهِ كَالْحَبْلِ وَالتَّوْكِيلِ}$$

80 and reach those parts which are difficult of access
with a cloth or the like – for example, a rope – or
have someone else do it:

$$\text{سُنَنُهُ مَضْمَضَةٌ غَسْلُ الْيَدَيْنِ} \qquad 81$$
$$\text{بَدْءًا وَالاسْتِنْشَاقُ ثُقْبَ الْأُذُنَيْنِ}$$

81 Its sunnas are rinsing the mouth, beginning (the
ghusl) by washing one's hands, sniffing up water
into the nose and wiping inside one's ear hole

$$\text{مَنْدُوبُهُ الْبَدْءُ بِغَسْلِهِ الْأَذَى} \qquad 82$$
$$\text{تَسْمِيَةٌ تَثْلِيثُ رَأْسِهِ كَذَا}$$

82 It is recommended to begin by washing away any
filth, to say the bismillah, to wash one's head
three times,

$$\text{تَقْدِيمُ أَعْضَاءِ الْوُضُوءِ قِلَّةُ مَا} \qquad 83$$
$$\text{بَدْءٌ بِأَعْلَى وَيَمِينٍ خُذْهُمَا}$$

83 to first wash the parts of the body (which one would
wash) for the wudu', use a little water, beginning
with the top and from the right, so take notice!

$$\text{تَبْدَأُ فِي الْغُسْلِ بِفَرْجٍ ثُمَّ كُفَّ} \quad 84$$
$$\text{عَنْ مَسِّهِ بِبَطْنٍ أَو جَنْبِ الْأَكُفّ}$$

84 Begin the ghusl by washing the private parts,
then avoid touching them with the palm (of the
hand) or the sides of (the palms)

$$\text{أَو إِصْبِعٍ ثُمَّ إِذَا مَسَسْتَهُ} \quad 85$$
$$\text{أَعِدْ مِنَ الْوُضُوء مَا فَعَلْتَهُ}$$

85 or the inside of the fingers, and if you do touch
them, then repeat that (part of the) wudu' you
have already done.

$$\text{مُوجِبُهُ حَيْضٌ نِفَاسٌ إِنْزَالُ} \quad 86$$
$$\text{مَغِيبُ كَمْرَةٍ بِفَرْجٍ إِنْجَالُ}$$

86 Ghusl becomes obligatory because of
menstruation, bleeding after childbirth,
emission of sperm, the penis penetrating the
vagina or penetration whatsoever.

$$\text{وَالأَوَّلَانِ مَنَعَا الْوَطْءَ إِلَى}$$

87

$$\text{غُسْلٍ وَالآخَرَانِ قُرْءَانَا جَلَا}$$

87 As for the first two, intercourse is forbidden until
the ghusl is made, and in the case of the last two,
recitation of the Qur'an is forbidden;

$$\text{وَالكُلُّ مَسْجِداً وَسَهْوُ الاغْتِسَالْ}$$

88

$$\text{مِثْلُ وُضُوئِكَ وَلَمْ تُعِدْ مُوَالْ}$$

88 and in the case of all four, entering the mosque
is forbidden. And if you have been negligent
(and have overlooked a part of the skin when
washing), then (make it up immediately) as in the
case of the wudu', but you do not have to repeat
washing the parts already washed after (what
you had omitted).

$$\text{التَّيَمُّمُ}$$

TAYAMMUM

$$\text{فَصْلٌ لِخَوْفِ ضُرٍّ أَوْ عَدَمِ مَا}$$

89

$$\text{عَوِّضْ مِنَ الطَّهَارَةِ التَّيَمُّمَا}$$

89 Section: if you fear illness or there is a lack of
water, then do tayammum instead of the (usual
purification)

وَصَلِّ فَرْضاً وَاحِداً وَإنْ تَصِلْ
جَنَازَةً وَسُنَّةً بِهِ يَحِلّ

90 and one may perform one *fard* salat, and if performed after this, then the *janaza* and sunna salats are permitted also.

وَجَازَ لِلنَّفْلِ ابْتِداً وَيَسْتَبِيح
الْفَرْضَ لَا الْجُمْعَةَ حَاضِرٌ صَحِيح

91

91 It is permitted to begin with *nafila* salats (when only *nafila* are performed) as (it is permitted to begin with) the *fard* salat, but not the jumu'a for the healthy person who is resident

فَرَائِضُ التَّيَمُّمُ

OBLIGATIONS OF TAYAMMUM

فُرُوضُهُ مَسْحُكَ وَجْهاً وَالْيَدَيْنِ
لِلْكُوعِ وَالنِّيَّةُ أُولَى الضَّرْبَتَيْنِ

92

92 The obligatory (aspects of *tayammum*) are to wipe one's face and hands up to the wrists, the intention, the first of two strikings (of the earth),

ثُمَّ الْمُوَالَاةُ صَعِيدٌ طَهُرَا
وَوَصْلُهَا بِهِ وَوَقْتُ حَضَرَا

93 (also obligatory is) performing the actions (of the tayammum) consecutively without interruption, using pure earth, performing the (tayammum) immediately before (the salat) and within the time (of the salat).

آخِرُهُ لِلرَّاجِي آيِسٌ فَقَطْ
أَوَّلُهُ وَالْمُتَرَدِّدُ الْوَسَطْ

94

94 One should delay it, if one hopes (to find water) and do it at the beginning (of the time) only if one has given up hope of finding it. If one finds oneself wavering between the two (states), then (perform it) in the middle (of the prescribed time for the salat).

سُنَنُ التَّيَمُّمِ

SUNNAS OF TAYAMMUM

سُنَنُهُ مَسْحُهُمَا لِلْمِرْفَقِ 95
وَضَرْبَةُ الْيَدَيْنِ تَرْتِيبٌ بَقِي

95 Its sunnas are wiping (one's forearms) up to the elbows, striking twice with the hands and observing the order.

مَنْدُوبُهُ تَسْمِيَةٌ وَصْفٌ حَمِيدْ 96
نَاقِضُهُ مِثْلُ الْوُضُوء وَيَزِيدْ

96 It is recommended to say the *bismillah* and (to wipe one's hands) in the praiseworthy manner. That which breaks the (*tayammum*) is the same (as that which breaks the) wudu' – with the additional (condition of)

وُجُودُ مَاءٍ قَبْلَ أَنْ صَلَّى وَإِنْ 97
بَعْدُ يَجِدْ يُعِدْ بِوَقْتٍ إِنْ يَكُنْ

97 the availability of water before doing the salat. If one finds (water) afterwards, then one repeats (the salat) within the time – (if one's state is)

نْكَائِفِ اللِّصِّ وَرَاجٍ قَدَّمَا

وَزَمِنٍ مُنَاوِلاً قَدْ عَدِمَا

98 like the person who fears (attack by) a thief, or
entertains hopes (of finding water) but who
nevertheless (does *tayammum*) before the final
time (and then finds water), or the person who is
physically incapable and who has no one to hand
him (the water).

كِتَابُ الصَّلَاةِ

THE BOOK OF SALAT

فَرَائِضُ الصَّلَاةِ

OBLIGATIONS OF THE SALAT

فَرَائِضُ الصَّلَاةِ سِتَّ عَشَرَةْ   ٩٩
شُرُوطُهَا أَرْبَعَةٌ مُفْتَقِرَةْ

99   There are sixteen *fard* obligations of the salat and
carrying them out is conditional upon four things
which must be complied with:

تَكْبِيرَةُ الْإِحْرَامِ وَالْقِيَامُ   ١٠٠
لَهَا وَنِيَّةٌ بِهَا تُرَامُ

100 the saying of Allahu akbar (which marks entry
into the salat and) its sanctity (by which all other
actions but the salat are excluded), the standing
for the (salat) and the intention;

$$\text{101} \quad \text{فَاتِحَةٌ مَعَ الْقِيَامِ وَالرُّكُوعْ}$$
$$\text{وَالرَّفْعُ مِنْهُ وَالسُّجُودُ بِالْخُضُوعْ}$$

101 (also obligatory is) the Fatiha done while standing
and the bowing, the return to standing position
after it, and prostration with submissiveness;

$$\text{102} \quad \text{وَالرَّفْعُ مِنْهُ وَالسَّلَامُ وَالْجُلُوسْ}$$
$$\text{لَهُ وَتَرْتِيبُ أَدَاءٍ فِي الْأُسُوسْ}$$

102 and (also obligatory is) raising (one's hands from
the ground), saying the salam, sitting for this
(salam), and the order of the *fard* elements when
performing these obligations,

$$\text{103} \quad \text{وَالِاعْتِدَالُ مُطْمَئِنًّا بِالْتِزَامْ}$$
$$\text{تَابَعَ مَأْمُومٌ بِإِحْرَامٍ سَلَامْ}$$

103 standing straight for a moment while relaxing
(the limbs) at the same time; those behind the
imam must perform the *takbiratu'l-ihram* and the
salam after him.

نِيَّتُهُ اقْتِدَاءٍ كَذَا الْإِمَامُ فِي
خَوْفٍ وَجَمْعٍ جُمْعَةٍ مُسْتَخْلَفٍ

104 One should make an intention to perform (the salat)
following (the imam); just as the imam should make
an intention in the 'fear' (salat), in joining (the two
salats), in the jumu'a and whenever standing in (for
the imam).

شَرْطُهَا الِاسْتِقْبَالُ طُهْرُ الْخَبَثِ
وَسَتْرُ عَوْرَةٍ وَطُهْرُ الْحَدَثِ

105 Its conditions are: facing the qibla, being clean
of filth, covering up the private parts and
purification from an impure state (*hadath*).

بِالذِّكْرِ وَالْقُدْرَةِ فِي غَيْرِ الْأَخِيرْ
تَفْرِيعُ نَاسِيهَا وَعَاجِزٌ كَثِيرْ

106 (All these conditions are necessary only) when
remembered and when one is capable – other
than in the last condition (i.e. purification from an
impure state which must be fulfilled in all cases).
As for the various (judgements) applicable in the
case of someone who forgets or who is incapable –
they are many in number.

نَدْبًا يُعِيدَانِ بِوَقْتٍ كَانْخَطَا

فِي قِبْلَةٍ لَا عَجْزِهَا أَوِ الْغِطَا

107 It is preferable in these two cases that the salat is repeated when within the time, similarly whenever one is mistaken in the direction of the qibla, but not in the case of incapacity (with respect to the qibla) or (when failing) to cover (one's private parts).

وَمَا عَدَا وَجْهَ وَكَفَّ الْحُرَّةِ   108

يَجِبُ سَتْرُهُ كَمَا فِي الْعَوْرَةِ

108 All of (the body of) a free woman must be covered, as the private parts, except the face and the palms.

لَكِنْ لَدَى كَشْفٍ لِصَدْرٍ أَوْ شَعَرْ   109

أَوْ طَرَفٍ تُعِيدُ فِي الْوَقْتِ الْمُقَرّْ

109 If the breast, the hair or another part of her body is uncovered, then she should repeat the salat in the prescribed time.

$$ \text{شَرْطُ وُجُوبِهَا النَّقَا مِنَ الدَّمِ} \qquad 110 $$

$$ \text{بِقَصَّةٍ أَوِ الْجُفُوفِ فَاعْلَمِ} $$

110 A condition of its being obligatory is her being free
of menstrual blood or of the whitish fluid (which
marks the end of the cycle), or becoming dry.

$$ \text{فَلَا قَضَا أَيَّامَهُ ثُمَّ دُخُولْ} \qquad 111 $$

$$ \text{وَقْتٍ فَأَدِّهَا بِهِ حَتْمًا أَقُولْ} $$

111 She does not have to make up her days (of
menstruation). The next (and final) condition is
that the time (of the salat) has arrived – in which
case I say: 'Be sure to perform it within this
(time)'.

$$ \text{سُنَنُ الصَّلَاةِ} $$

SUNNAS OF SALAT

$$ \text{سُنَنُهَا السُّورَةُ بَعْدَ الْوَاقِيَةْ} \qquad 112 $$

$$ \text{مَعَ الْقِيَامِ أَوَّلاً وَالثَّانِيَةْ} $$

112 Its sunna are the sura after al-Waqiya (the Fatiha)
– the Shield – together with the standing both for
the first and the second,

$$\text{جَهْرٌ وَسِرٌّ بِمَحَلٍّ لَهُمَا} \qquad 113$$
$$\text{تَكْبِيرُهُ إِلَّا الَّذِي تَقَدَّمَا}$$

113 (reciting) out loud or to oneself – in accordance
   with the particular salat, the saying of the *takbir*
   except that mentioned above (which is *fard*),

$$\text{كُلُّ تَشَهُّدٍ جُلُوسٌ أَوَّلُ} \qquad 114$$
$$\text{وَالثَّانِي لَا مَا لِلسَّلَامِ يَحْصُلُ}$$

114 each *tashahhud*, the first and second sitting – except
   for the part of it in which the salam is said (which is
   fard),

$$\text{وَسَمِعَ اللَّهُ لِمَنْ حَمِدَهْ} \qquad 115$$
$$\text{فِي الرَّفْعِ مِنْ رُكُوعِهِ أَوْرَدَهْ}$$

115 and the saying *sami'Allahu liman hamida* (Allah
   hears him who praises Him) on rising from the
   bowing – all of the above are (*mu'akkad*) sunnas

$$\text{اَلْفَذُّ وَالْإِمَامُ هَذَا أُكِّدَا} \quad 116$$
$$\text{وَالْبَاقِي كَالْمَنْدُوبِ فِي الْحُكْمِ بَدَا}$$

116 of particular importance, that is in the case
of the person praying alone and the imam,
while the following sunnas are (only *mandoub*)
recommended, and as such their judgement
(does not require a prostration of negligence if
omitted),

$$\text{إِقَامَةٌ سُجُودُهُ عَلَى الْيَدَيْنِ} \quad 117$$
$$\text{وَطَرَفُ الرِّجْلَيْنِ مِثْلُ الرُّكْبَتَيْنِ}$$

117 (namely) the *iqama*, prostrating on both hands and
on the ends of the feet and on the knees,

$$\text{إِنْصَاتُ مُقْتَدٍ بِجَهْرٍ ثُمَّ رَدّْ} \quad 118$$
$$\text{عَلَى الْإِمَامِ وَالْيَسَارِ وَأَحَدْ}$$

118 the person following (the imam) should listen to
what (is recited) aloud, then answer (silently) the
(salam of the) imam, and the person to the left if
there is someone (there),

$$\text{بِهِ وَزَائِدُ سُكُونٍ لِلْحُضُورْ}$$

$$\text{سُتْرَةُ غَيْرِ مُقْتَدٍ خَافَ الْمُرُورْ}$$

119

119 prolonging the 'sitting still a moment' in order to be present, placing a *sutra* – in the case of someone not following (the imam), if he fears someone will pass in front of him,

$$\text{جَهْرُ السَّلَامِ كَلِمُ التَّشَهُّدِ}$$

$$\text{وَأَنْ يُصَلَّى عَلَى مُحَمَّدِ}$$

120

120 saying the salam aloud, the (particular) wording of the *tashahhud*, and the prayer on Muhammad.

$$\text{الْأَذَانُ}$$

THE ADHAN

$$\text{سُنَّ الْأَذَانُ لِجَمَاعَةٍ أَتَتْ}$$

$$\text{فَرْضاً بِوَقْتِهِ وَغَيْراً طَلَبَتْ}$$

121

121 The *adhan* for the *fard* salat performed in the *jama'a* – in order to call others to it – is a(nother) sunna, when the time comes,

$$\text{وَقَصْرُ مَنْ سَافَرَ أَرْبَعَ بُرُدْ} \quad 122$$
$$\text{ظُهْراً عِشاً عَصْراً إِلَى حِينِ يَعُدْ}$$

122 shortening the salat for the traveller for a distance
of four *bareeds* (of each 12 Arab miles[1]), for dhuhr,
'isha and 'asr until he returns

$$\text{مِمَّا وَرَا السُّكْنَى إِلَيْهِ إِنْ قَدِمْ} \quad 123$$
$$\text{مُقِيمُ أَرْبَعَةِ أَيَّامٍ يَتِمّْ}$$

123 to within (the confines of) a settled place as long
as he does not intend to stay somewhere (on his
journey) for more than four days, in which case
he does the salat in full.

مَنْدُوبَاتُ الصَّلَاةِ

RECOMMENDED ACTS OF THE SALAT

$$\text{مَنْدُوبُهَا تَيَامُنٌ مَعَ السَّلَامْ} \quad 124$$
$$\text{تَأْمِينُ مَنْ صَلَّى عَدَا جَهْرِ الْإِمَامْ}$$

124 It is recommended to turn the head to the right
when saying the (final) salam; and for the person
performing the salat to say amin (silently), but not
for the imam (after) reciting (the Fatiha) aloud;

---

1   Each 'Arab' mile is 1973 metres; 48 miles would be just over 90 km

وَقَوْلُ رَبَّنَا لَكَ الْحَمْدُ عَدَا ١٢٥

مَنْ أَمَّ وَالْقُنُوتُ فِي الصُّبْحِ بَدَا

125 and the saying *rabbana laka'l-hamd*, but not for the
imam; and the *qunut* for the salat of subh;

رِدًا وَتَسْبِيحُ السُّجُودِ وَالرُّكُوعْ ١٢٦

سَدْلُ يَدٍ تَكْبِيرُهُ مَعَ الشُّرُوعْ

126 the wearing of a cloak; the saying of 'subhanallah...'
during the prostration and the bowing, letting
one's arms hang by one's side, saying Allahu
akbar when beginning (the movements of the
salat),

وَبَعْدَ أَنْ يَقُومَ مِنْ وُسْطَاهُ ١٢٧

وَعَقْدُهُ الثَّلَاثَ مِنْ يُمْنَاهُ

127 and after getting up from the middle (sitting, after
his second *rak'at*), clenching the three smaller
fingers of his right hand

لَدَى التَّشَهُّدِ وَبَسْطُ مَا خَلَاهُ ١٢٨

تَحْرِيكُ سَبَّابَتِهَا حِينَ تَلَاهُ

128 when saying the *tashahhud* while letting the other
(two fingers) remain straight, and moving one's
index finger while saying (the *tashahhud*);

$$وَالْبَطْنُ مِنْ نَخِذِ رِجَالٌ يُبْعِدُونْ \qquad 129$$

$$وَمِرْفَقًا مِنْ رُكْبَةٍ إِذْ يَسْجُدُونْ$$

129 the belly should not touch the thigh of a man, nor
the elbow his knee when prostrating;

$$وَصِفَةُ الْجُلُوسِ تَمْكِينُ الْيَدِ \qquad 130$$

$$مِنْ رُكْبَتَيْهِ فِي الرُّكُوعِ وَزِدْ$$

130 the specific way of sitting (for the *tashahhud*);
placing the hands firmly on the knees for the
ruku', and also

$$نَصْبُهُمَا قِرَاءَةُ الْمَأْمُومِ فِي \qquad 131$$

$$سِرِّيَّةٍ وَضْعُ الْيَدَيْنِ فَاقْتَفِي$$

131 his knees should be straight (during the bowing);
the person behing the imam reciting (to himself)
whenever (the imam recites) silently, placing the
hands level with the ears

$$لَدَى السُّجُودِ حَذْوَ أُذْنٍ وَكَذَا \qquad 132$$

$$رَفْعُ الْيَدَيْنِ عِنْدَ الْإِحْرَامِ خُذَا$$

132 in the prostration, and likewise, raising the hands
for the *takbiratu'l-ihram*.

$$\text{تَطْوِيلُهُ صُبْحاً وَظُهْراً سُورَتَيْنِ} \qquad 133$$
$$\text{تَوَسُّطُ الْعِشَا وَقَصْرُ الْبَاقِيَيْنِ}$$

133 He should recite long suras in the subh and dhuhr salats, medium length ones at 'isha, and shorter ones for the two other salats,

$$\text{كَالسُّورَةِ الْأُخْرَى كَذَا الْوُسْطَى اسْتُحِبّ} \qquad 134$$
$$\text{سَبْقُ يَدٍ وَضْعاً وَفِي الرَّفْعِ الرُّكَبْ}$$

134 likewise, recite a shorter sura in the second *rak'at*; it is recommended, too, to shorten the sitting in the middle (of the salat), and to put one's hands on the ground first (going into sajda) but to first raise the knees when rising.

مَكْرُوهَاتُ الصَّلَاةِ

MAKRUH ACTS IN THE SALAT

$$\text{وَكَرِهُوا بَسْمَلَةً تَعَوُّذاً} \qquad 135$$
$$\text{فِي الْفَرْضِ وَالسُّجُودَ فِي الثَّوْبِ كَذَا}$$

135 And they have deemed *makruh* the bismillah, saying *a'oudhu billahi* – I seek refuge – in the *fard* salat, and prostrating on cloth,

$$\text{كَوْرُ عِمَامَةٍ وَبَعْضُ كُمِّهِ} \quad 136$$
$$\text{وَحَمْلُ شَيْءٍ فِيهِ أَوْ فِي فَمِهْ}$$

136 the fold of the turban or part of the sleeve or
carrying something in it or one's mouth,

$$\text{قِرَاءَةٌ لَدَى السُّجُودِ وَالرُّكُوعْ} \quad 137$$
$$\text{تَفَكُّرُ الْقَلْبِ بِمَا نَافَى الْخُشُوعْ}$$

137 reciting during the prostration or the bowing,
allowing the heart to think about anything which
humility,

$$\text{وَعَبَثٌ وَالِالْتِفَاتُ وَالدُّعَا} \quad 138$$
$$\text{أَثْنَاءَ قِرَاءَةٍ كَذَا إِنْ رَكَعَا}$$

138 and (absent minded) play, turning (away from the
qibla) and making du'a during the recitation, and
likewise in the bowing,

$$\text{تَشْبِيكٌ أَوْ فَرْقَعَةُ الأَصَابِعْ} \quad 139$$
$$\text{تَخَصُّرُ تَغْمِيضُ عَيْنٍ تَابِعْ}$$

139 interlocking or cracking the fingers, placing one's
hands on the hip (when standing), closing one's
eyes.

140 فَصْلُ وَخَمْسُ صَلَوَاتٍ فَرْضُ عَيْنْ

وَهْيَ كِفَايَةٌ لِمَيِّتٍ دُونَ مَيْنْ

140 Section: and the five prayers are a *fard* obligation,
and (the salat) over the dead person is a communal
responsibility, without doubt

141 فُرُوضُهَا التَّكْبِيرُ أَرْبَعاً دُعَا

وَنِيَّةٌ سَلَامُ سِرٍّ تَبِعَا

141 Its *fard* obligations are the *takbir* four times, the
du'a, the intention, and saying the salam silently

142 وَكَالصَّلَاةِ أَلْغُسْلُ دَفْنُ وَكَفَنْ

وِتْرُ كُسُوفُ عِيدُ إِسْتِسْقَا سُنَنْ

142 and like the salat, the ghusl, burial and enshrouding
the corpse [are communal responsibilities] while
the witr, eclipse, Eid and rain salat are sunnas.

143 فَجْرُ رَغِيبَةٌ وَتُقْضَى لِلزَّوَالْ
وَالْفَرْضُ يُقْضَى أَبَداً وِبِالتَّوَالْ

143 fajr is a (particularly) desired (sunna) and can be made up right up to the sun's zenith. However, the obligatory must be made up however long the delay, and in its order.

144 نُدِبَ نَفْلٌ مُطْلَقاً وَأُكِّدَتْ
تَحِيَّةٌ ضُحًى تَرَاوِيحُ تَلَتْ

144 It is recommended to do the *nafila* at all times, although particular importance is attached to the salat of greeting, the mid-morning salat and the tarawih.

145 وَقَبْلَ وِتْرٍ مِثْلَ ظُهْرٍ عَصْرِ
وَبَعْدَ مَغْرِبٍ وَبَعْدَ ظُهْرِ

145 (*Nafila* salats are performed) before the witr, before dhuhr and 'asr, and after maghrib and after dhuhr.

PROSTRATIONS FOR FORGETFULNESS

لِنَقْصِ سُنَّةٍ سَهْواً يُسَنّ   146

قَبْلَ السَّلَامِ سَجْدَتَانِ أَوْ سُنَنْ

146 If one or more sunnas are missed out of negligence,
two prostrations should be made before the salam
('alaykum)

إِنْ أُكِّدَتْ وَمَنْ يَزِدْ سَهْواً سَجَدْ   147

بَعْدُ كَذَا وَالنَّقْصَ غَلِّبْ إِنْ وَرَدْ

147 in the case of *mu'akkad* sunnas; anyone who does
something extra, should prostrate after this; if he
misses something (and does something extra), it is
his missing something which counts;

وَاسْتَدْرِكِ الْقَبْلِيَّ مَعَ قُرْبِ السَّلَامْ   148

وَاسْتَدْرِكِ الْبَعْدِيَّ وَلَوْ مِنْ بَعْدِ عَامْ

148 if one forgets a prostration owing before (the
salam), then it is made good (afterwards) – if little
time has elapsed after saying the salam; if one
forgets such a prostration after (the salam), then it
is to be made good – even after a year.

عَنْ مُقْتَدٍ يَحْمِلُ هَذَيْنِ الإِمَامْ

وَبَطَلَتْ بِعَمْدِ نَفْخٍ أَوْ كَلَامْ

149 The imam bears the responsibility (i.e. for what has been missed or any addition) – both (what has been missed or any addition) – and not those following him; and the salat is invalidated if one deliberately for blowing out (air excessively) or speaking.

لِغَيْرِ إِصْلَاحٍ وَبِالْمُشْغِلِ عَنْ

فَرْضٍ وَفِي الْوَقْتِ أَعِدْ إِذَا يُسَنُّ

150 for a reason other than to correct (the imam), and anything (like colic for example) which distracts from performing the *fard* (aspects invalidates the salat); and if from (one of) the sunna (aspects), one should repeat it, if still within the time;

وَحَدَثٍ وَسَهْوِ زَيْدِ الْمِثْلِ

قَهْقَهَةٍ وَعَمْدِ شُرْبٍ أَكْلِ

151 if his purity is broken in any way, or he inadvertently makes an addition (of a further two *rak'ats*) the like (of which he has already performed – i.e. for the subh), or he guffaws or deliberately eats or drinks (something)

$$\text{وَسَجْدَةٍ فِي ءٍ وَذِكْرٍ فَرْضِ}$$
$$\text{أَقَلَّ مِنْ سِتٍّ كَذِكْرِ الْبَعْضِ}$$

152 or does an (extra) prostration (deliberately), or vomits (and deliberately swallows his vomit again) or remembers missed *fard* (salats as long as they amount to) less than six, or part (of a salat – all invalidate the current salat),

$$\text{وَفَوْتِ قَبْلِيّ ثَلَاثَ سُنَنِ}$$
$$\text{بِفَصْلِ مَسْجِدٍ كَطُولِ الزَّمَنِ}$$

153 or (recalling) omitting a prostration (of negligence) which one should have done before the salam (of a previous salat) to make good three missed sunnas – if one has left the mosque or a long time has elapsed.

$$\text{وَاسْتَدْرِكِ الرُّكْنَ فَإِنْ حَالَ الرُّكُوعْ}$$
$$\text{فَأَلْغِ ذَاتَ السَّهْوِ وَالْبِنَا يَطُوعْ}$$

154 (If one remembers missing) any obligatory part (of the salat one is currently performing), one should put it right there and then, but if one has already gone into the bowing, then one treats as annulled the *rak'at* containing the omission and carries on (the rest of the prayer) basing it on what one has done previous to this (annulled *rak'at*).

$$\text{كَفِعْلِ مَنْ سَلَّمَ لكِنْ يُحْرِمُ} \qquad 155$$
$$\text{لِلْبَاقِي وَالطُّولُ الْفَسَادَ مُلْزِمُ}$$

155 Anyone who (remembers only after) making the
salam should do likewise, although he must say
Allahu akbar for the rest; but if a long time has
elapsed, then this invalidates (his salat)

$$\text{مَنْ شَكَّ فِي رُكْنٍ بَنَى عَلَى الْيَقِينْ} \qquad 156$$
$$\text{وَلْيَسْجُدُوا الْبَعْدِيَّ لكِنْ قَدْ يَبِينْ}$$

156 Whoever has doubts regarding an obligation
should resume from where he is certain, and then
prostrate after the salaam; and if an imperfection
occurs

$$\text{لِأَنْ بَنَوْا فِي فِعْلِهِمْ وَالْقَوْلِي} \qquad 157$$
$$\text{نَقْصٌ بِفَوْتِ سُورَةٍ فَالْقَبْلِي}$$

157 because he omits the sura after the Umm al-
Qur'an when resuming from the actions and
spoken elements (of the salat which he knows)
to be correct then he should do the prostration
before the salam;

كَذَاكِرِ الْوُسْطَى وَالْأَيْدِي قَدْ رَفَعْ

ورُكباً لَا قَبْلَ ذَا لكِنْ رَجَعْ

158

158 likewise, the person who has already raised his
hands and knees and who remembers (having
omitted) the middle (sitting and does not return
to the sitting position should prostrate before the
salam), but does not (prostrate) if he returns (to
the sitting position) before (raising his hands and
knees).

صَلَاةُ الْجُمُعَة

LAWS GOVERNING THE JUMU'A

فَصْلٌ بِمَوْطِنِ الْقُرَى قَدْ فُرِضَتْ

صَلَاةُ جُمْعَةٍ لِخُطْبَةٍ تَلَتْ

159

159 The salat of jumu'a following a khutba is obligatory
in towns and settlements

بِجَامِعٍ عَلَى مُقِيمٍ مَا انْعَذَرْ

حُرٍّ قَرِيبٍ بِكَفَرْسَخٍ ذَكَرْ

160

160 in a jami' mosque. It is obligatory for the resident
without a valid excuse, who is free, and who lives
nearby – that is, within three miles[2], and who is male;

2   *farsakh*:12,000 cubits, corresponding roughly to three miles

وَأَجْزَأَتْ غَيْراً نَعَمْ قَدْ تُنْدَبُ ١٦١
عِنْدَ التِّدَا السَّعْىُ إِلَيْهَا يَجِبُ

161 If, however, other than these (persons who are
under an obligation to) perform it, then it is
accepted of them (and counts instead of dhuhr),
indeed it is recommended. And when the call is
made, one must make haste to it.

وَسُنَّ غَسْلٌ بِالرَّوَاحِ اتَّصَلَا ١٦٢
وَنُدِبَ تَهْجِيرٌ وَحَالٌ جَمُلَا

162 It is a sunna to make a ghusl and to make it
immediately before leaving (for the mosque). It is
recommended to set out in the midday heat, to
be well-groomed and neat of appearance.

بِجُمْعَةٍ جَمَاعَةٌ قَدْ وَجَبَتْ ١٦٣
سُنَّتْ بِفَرْضٍ وَبِرَكْعَةٍ رَسَتْ

163 It is obligatory to have a *jama'a* for the jumu'a
whereas it is (only) a sunna for the *fard* salat,
and the (excellence of this *jama'a*) is obtained by
catching (at least) one *rak'at*.

$$\text{وَنُدِبَتْ إِعَادَةُ ٱلْفَذِّ بِهَا} \quad 164$$
$$\text{لَا مَغْرِباً كَذَا عِشًا مُوتِرُهَا}$$

164 It is recommended that the person who has prayed
alone (at home) repeat (the salat) with the *jama'a*,
but not in the case of maghrib or the 'isha – when
followed by its witr.

شُرُوطُ الْإِمَامِ

CONDITIONS FOR THE IMAM

$$\text{شَرْطُ الْإِمَامِ ذَكَرٌ مُكَلَّفُ} \quad 165$$
$$\text{آتٍ بِالْأَرْكَانِ وَحُكْمًا يَعْرِفُ}$$

165 An imam must fulfil the conditions of being
male and *mukallaf* (that is, of age and sane), be
(physically) capable of performing the *fard* aspects
of the salat and know the judgements (pertaining
to the salat),

$$\text{وَغَيْرُ ذِي فِسْقٍ وَلَحْنٍ وَأُقْتِدَا} \quad 166$$
$$\text{فِي جُمْعَةٍ حُرٌّ مِقِيمٌ عُدِّدَا}$$

166 and must not be corrupt, or someone who
mispronounces, nor (himself) be following
(another imam in front of him); and regarding
the jumu'a, be free and resident.

$$وِيُكْرَهُ السَّلَسُ وَالقُرُوحُ مَعْ \qquad 167$$
$$بَادٍ لِغَيْرِهِمْ وَمَنْ يُكْرَهُ دَعْ$$

167 It is makruh in the case of someone with
incontinence, or with sores, or when a Bedouin
serves as an imam for others, and desist from
(performing the salat behind) someone if people
dislike him (as imam);

$$وَكَالأَشَلِّ وَإِمَامَةٍ بِلَا \qquad 168$$
$$رِداً بِمَسْجِدٍ صَلَاةٌ تُجْتَلَى$$

168 likewise, a person whose arm is paralysed (or
amputated), or not wearing a cloak when imam
in a mosque, or when a (row of the) salat is

$$بَيْنَ الأَسَاطِينِ وَقُدَّامَ الإِمَامْ \qquad 169$$
$$جَمَاعَةٌ بَعْدَ صَلَاةٍ ذِي الْتِزَامْ$$

169 interrupted by columns, or (standing) in front of
the imam, or performing another *jama'a* after the
regular *jama'a*;

$$\text{وَرَاتِبٌ مَجْهُولٌ أَوْ مَنْ أَبَنَا} \quad 170$$
$$\text{وَأَغْلَفُ عَبْدٌ خَصِيٌّ ابْنُ زِنَا}$$

170 (likewise) appointing a regular imam who is (as yet) unknown, or someone who is blameworthy, uncircumcised, a slave, a eunuch or a bastard.

$$\text{وَجَازَ عِنِّينٌ وَأَعْمَى أَلْكَنُ} \quad 171$$
$$\text{مَجَذَّمٌ خَفَّ وَهَذَا الْمُمْكِنُ}$$

171 It is permitted in the case of an impotent man, a blind man, someone with a speech impediment or afflicted by leprosy, as long as slight — and this is enough (for our purposes here).

$$\text{وَالْمُقْتَدِي الْإِمَامَ يَتْبَعُ خَلَا} \quad 172$$
$$\text{زِيَادَةً قَدْ حُقِّقَتْ عَنْهَا لَا}$$

172 The person behind (the imam) must imitate the imam except if the latter makes an addition — and the person following him is certain of this — in which case he does not do it.

$$173 \qquad \text{وَأَحْرَمَ الْمَسْبُوقُ فَوْراً وَدَخَلْ}$$
$$\text{مَعَ الْإِمَامِ كَــيْفَمَا كَانَ الْعَمَلْ}$$

173 The person who arrives late (for the *jama'a*) should make the *takbiratu'l-ihram* immediately and join the salat with the imam – whatever his position or movement –

$$174 \qquad \text{مُكَبِّراً إِنْ سَاجِداً أَوْ رَاكِعَا}$$
$$\text{أَلْفَاهُ لَا فِي جَلْسَةٍ وَتَابَعَا}$$

174 saying 'Allahu akbar', if joining him in the act of prostration or bowing, but not in the sitting, and should then follow (the imam).

$$175 \qquad \text{إِنْ سَلَّمَ الْإِمَامُ قَامَ قَاضِيَا}$$
$$\text{أَقْوَالَهُ وَفِي الْأَفْعَالِ بَانِيَا}$$

175 When the imam says the (final) salaam, he must get up to make up for the spoken aspects (of the salat) but must carry on with the movements from where he joined (the *jama'a*).

كَبَّرَ إِنْ حَصَّلَ شَفْعاً أَوْ أَقَلّ   176
مِنْ رَكْعَةٍ وَالسَّهْوَ إِذْ ذَاكَ احْتَمَلْ

176   He must say the Allahu akbar (when standing up
after the imam's salam) if he completes a pair (of
rak'ats) or less than a *rak'at*; and in the case of (the
ma'mum's) negligence, (while behind) the imam
(then the latter) is responsible.

وَيَسْجُدُ الْمَسْبُوقُ قَبْلِيَّ الإِمَامْ   177
مَعْهُ وَبَعْدِياً قَضَى بَعْدَ السَّلَامْ

177   The person who joins (the salat) late should make
the (prostration of negligence) which has to be
done before the salam with the imam; that to be
done after, he should make up after the salam,

أَدْرَكَ ذَاكَ السَّهْوَ أَوْ لَا قَيَّدُوا   178
مَنْ لَمْ يُحَصِّلْ رَكْعَةً لَا يَسْجُدُ

178   irrespective of whether he was present if (the
imam) was negligent, although the (fuqaha) have
stipulated that if he did not catch a *rak'at*, then he
does not do any prostration (of negligence with
the imam).

وَبَطَلَتْ لِمُقْتَدٍ بِمُبْطِلِ
عَلَى الْإِمَامِ غَيْرَ فَرْعٍ مُنْجَلِي

179 The salat is invalidated for those behind the
imam when that of the latter is invalidated, other
than in one obvious case:

مَنْ ذَكَرَ الْحَدَثَ أَوْ بِهِ غُلِبْ
إِنْ بَادَرَ الْخُرُوجَ مِنْهَا وَنُدِبْ

180

180 if the imam remembers that he is in a state of
ritual impurity or is overcome by ritual impurity
(during the salat) – as long as he leaves the salat
immediately. In this case it is recommended

تَقْدِيمُ مُؤْتَمٍّ يُتِمُّ بِهِمُو
فَإِنْ أَبَاهُ انْفَرَدُوا أَوْ قَدَّمُوا

181

181 that he designate one of those following him to
complete the salat for them; if he refuses, then they
may complete it individually or may themselves
put someone forward (to lead the salat).

كِتَابُ الزَّكَاةِ

THE BOOK OF ZAKAT

فُرِضَتِ الزَّكَاةُ فِيمَا يُرْتَسَمْ 182
عَيْنٍ وَحَبٍّ وَثِمَارٍ وَنَعَمْ

182 Zakat is a *fard* obligation on everything which has
been laid down (in the shari'ah): gold and silver,
grains and fruit, and grazing livestock.

فِى ٱلْعَيْنِ وَالْأَنْعَامِ حَقَّتْ كُلَّ عَامْ 183
يَكْمُلُ وَالْحَبُّ بِالْإِفْرَاكِ يُرَامْ

183 It becomes due on gold and silver and livestock
after a full (lunar) year, on grains when they
become firm and may be separated from the ears,

وَالتَّمْرُ وَالزَّبِيبُ بِالطِّيبِ وَفِي 184
ذِي الزَّيْتِ مِنْ زَيْتِهِ وَٱلْحَبُّ يَفِي

184 on dates and raisins when they ripen, and on the
oil from oil-bearing seeds – if they amount to the
nisab (minimum legal amount).

كِتَابُ الزَّكَاةِ

THE BOOK OF ZAKAT

فُرِضَتِ الزَّكَاةُ فِيمَا يُرْتَسَمْ   182

عَيْنٍ وَحَبٍّ وَثِمَارٍ وَنَعَمْ

182 Zakat is a *fard* obligation on everything which has
been laid down (in the shari'ah): gold and silver,
grains and fruit, and grazing livestock.

فِى ٱلعَيْنِ وَالْأَنْعَامِ حَقَّتْ كُلَّ عَامْ   183

يَكْمُلُ والْحَبُّ بِالْإِفْرَاكِ يُرَامْ

183 It becomes due on gold and silver and livestock
after a full (lunar) year, on grains when they
become firm and may be separated from the ears,

وَالتَّمْرُ وَالزَّبِيبُ بِالطِّيبِ وَفِي   184

ذِي الزَّيْتِ مِنْ زَيْتِهِ وَالْحَبُّ يَفِي

184 on dates and raisins when they ripen, and on the
oil from oil-bearing seeds – if they amount to the
nisab (minimum legal amount).

$$\text{وَبَطَلَتْ لُمُقْتَدٍ بِمُبْطِلِ}$$
$$\text{عَلَى الْإِمَامِ غَيْرَ فَرْعٍ مُنْجَلِي}$$

179 The salat is invalidated for those behind the
imam when that of the latter is invalidated, other
than in one obvious case:

$$\text{مَنْ ذَكَرَ الْحَدَثَ أَوْ بِهِ غُلِبْ}$$
$$\text{إِنْ بَادَرَ الْخُرُوجَ مِنْهَا وَنُدِبْ}$$

180

180 if the imam remembers that he is in a state of
ritual impurity or is overcome by ritual impurity
(during the salat) – as long as he leaves the salat
immediately. In this case it is recommended

$$\text{تَقْدِيمُ مُؤْتَمٍّ يُتِمُّ بِهِمُو}$$
$$\text{فَإِنْ أَبَاهُ انْفَرَدُوا أَوْ قَدَّمُوا}$$

181

181 that he designate one of those following him to
complete the salat for them; if he refuses, then they
may complete it individually or may themselves
put someone forward (to lead the salat).

$$\text{وَهِيَ فِي الثِّمَارِ وَالْحَبِّ الْعُشْرُ} \quad 185$$
$$\text{أَوْ نِصْفُهُ إِنْ آلَةُ السَّقْيِ يَجُرَّ}$$

185 There is a tenth to pay on fruit and grains, or the half of this if a means of irrigation has been employed.

$$\text{خَمْسَةُ أَوْسُقٍ نِصَابٌ فِيهِمَا} \quad 186$$
$$\text{فِي فِضَّةٍ قُلْ مِائَتَانِ دِرْهَمَا}$$

186 The *nisab* – the legal zakatable amount – is five *wasqs*, on silver at least two hundred dirhams.

$$\text{عِشْرُونَ دِينَاراً نِصَابٌ فِي الذَّهَبْ} \quad 187$$
$$\text{وَرُبْعُ الْعُشْرِ فِيهِمَا وَجَبْ}$$

187 The *nisab* for gold is twenty dinars – of which two and a half percent is due on both (gold and silver),

$$\text{وَالْعَرْضُ ذُو التَّجْرِ وَدَيْنُ مَنْ أَدَارْ} \quad 188$$
$$\text{قِيمَتُهَا كَالْعَيْنِ ثُمَّ ذُو احْتِكَارْ}$$

188 and on goods for trade, and on a credit incurred (as capital) to buy and sell (on a daily basis), and the amount due is the same as gold and silver; it is also due on anything stocked (for sale later, when market conditions are favourable).

$$
\text{زَكَّى لِقَبْضِ ثَمَنٍ أَوْ دَيْنٍ}
$$
$$
\text{عَيْناً بِشَرْطِ الْحَوْلِ لِلْأَصْلَيْنِ}
$$

189 The zakat is paid in gold or silver when taking
possession of the price (for the sale of the goods),
or of the credit incurred as capital, on condition
that the year has elapsed on the two.

$$
\text{زَكَاةُ الْمَوَاشِي}
$$

ZAKAT OF LIVESTOCK

$$
\text{فِي كُلِّ خَمْسَةٍ جِمَالٌ جَذَعَةٌ}
$$
$$
\text{مِنْ غَنَمٍ بِنْتُ الْمَخَاضِ مُقْنِعَةٌ}
$$

190

190 On every five camels, a sheep or goat of two
years (is to be paid); a she-camel in its second
year

$$
\text{فِي الْخَمْسِ وَالْعِشْرِينَ وَابْنَةُ اللَّبُونْ}
$$
$$
\text{فِي سِتَّةٍ مَعَ الثَّلَاثِينَ تَكُونْ}
$$

191

191 is enough on twenty-five camels; on thirty-six
camels, one she-camel in its third year;

$$\text{سِتًّا وَأَرْبَعِينَ حِقَّةٌ كَفَتْ}$$
$$\text{جَذْعَةُ إِحْدَى وَسِتِّينَ وَفَتْ}$$

192

192 on forty six, a she-camel of four years is enough;
on sixty-one, a she-camel of five years;

$$\text{بِنْتَا لَبُونٍ سِتَّةً وَسَبْعِينْ}$$
$$\text{وَحِقَّتَانِ وَاحِداً وَتِسْعِينْ}$$

193

193 on seventy-six, two she-camels of three years
old; on ninety-one, two she-camels of four years
old;

$$\text{وَمَعْ ثَلَاثِينَ ثَلَاثٌ أَيْ بَنَاتْ}$$
$$\text{لَبُونٍ أَوْ خُذْ حِقَّتَيْنِ بِافْتِيَاتْ}$$

194

194 on every thirty over a hundred, three she-camels
of three years or two she-camels of four years,
according to the assessment (of the tax-collector).

$$\text{إِذَا الثَّلَاثِينَ تَلَتْهَا الْمِائَةُ}$$
$$\text{فِي كُلِّ خَمْسِينَ كَمَالاً حِقَّةُ}$$

195

195 This is only if the total is one hundred and thirty;
on every fifty (over a hundred), a she-camel of
four years;

196 وَكُلُّ أَرْبَعِينَ بِنْتُ لَبُونْ
وَهَكَذَا مَا زَادَ أَمْرُهُ يَهُونْ

196 on every forty, a she-camel of three years, and so on.

197 عِجْلٌ تَبِيعٌ فِي ثَلَاثِينَ بَقَرْ
مُسِنَّةٌ فِي أَرْبَعِينَ تُسْتَطَرْ

197 on thirty cows, a two year old cow (is paid), on forty a three year old,

198 وَهَكَذَا مَا ارْتَفَعَتْ ثُمَّ الْغَنَمْ
شَاةٌ لِأَرْبَعِينَ مَعَ أُخْرَى تُضَمّْ

198 and so on. As for sheep or goats, one sheep or goat is paid on forty, and then another is added

199 فِي وَاحِدٍ عِشْرِينَ يَتْلُو وَمِئَةْ
وَمَعْ ثَمَانِينَ ثَلَاثٌ مُجْزِئَةْ

199 when one hundred and twenty one is reached; three is enough with eighty more (i.e. on two hundred and one upwards);

$$\text{وَأَرْبَعاً خُذْ مِنْ مِئِينَ أَرْبَع} \quad 200$$

$$\text{شَاةٌ لِكُلِّ مِائَةٍ إِنْ تُرْفَع}$$

200 take four on four hundred, and then one sheep
for every hundred from then on.

$$\text{وَحَوْلُ الْأَرْبَاحِ وَنَسْلٍ كَالْأُصُولْ} \quad 201$$

$$\text{وَالطَّارِ لَا عَمَّا يُزَكَّى أَنْ يَحُولْ}$$

201 The *hawl* (elapsing of the lunar year) on any profit
or offspring is as the original (capital or livestock),
but the 'year' has to elapse on anything suddenly
acquired (as a gift, sale or inheritance, if – when
added to other wealth in one's possession below
the *nisab* – the total amounts to the *nisab*) –
although if zakat is already due on what (is in
one's possession as the *nisab* has been reached
and some sudden acquisition is added to it) then
no (further) elapsing of a year (is necessary).

$$\text{وَلَا يُزَكَّى وَقَصٌ مِنَ النَّعَمْ} \quad 202$$

$$\text{كَذَاكَ مَا دُونَ النِّصَابِ وَلْيَعُمّ}$$

202 No (extra) zakat is paid on amounts which (are
above one rate but which) fall short of the (next)
rate of livestock, nor on anything below the *nisab*
in general,

$$\text{وَعَسَلٌ فَاكِهَةٌ مَعَ الْخُضَرْ} \qquad 203$$
$$\text{إِذْ هِيَ فِي الْمُقْتَاتِ مِمَّا يُدَّخَرْ}$$

203 nor on honey, soft fruit and vegetables – for zakat is paid on storable, basic commodities.

$$\text{وَيَحْصُلُ النِّصَابُ مِنْ صِنْفَيْنِ} \qquad 204$$
$$\text{كَذَهَبٍ وَفِضَّةٍ مِنْ عَيْنٍ}$$

204 The *nisab* may be reached by (putting together) two kinds (of zakatable items), like gold and silver in the case of money,

$$\text{وَالضَّأْنُ لِلْمَعْزِ وَبُخْتٌ لِلْعِرَابْ} \qquad 205$$
$$\text{وَبَقَرٌ إِلَى الْجَوَامِيسِ اصْطِحَابْ}$$

205 or (putting) sheep with goats, Bactrian with Arabian camels, cows with water buffalo,

$$\text{وَالْقَمْحُ لِلشَّعِيرِ لِلسُّلْتِ يُصَارْ} \qquad 206$$
$$\text{كَذَا الْقَطَانِي وَالزَّبِيبُ وَالثِّمَارْ}$$

206 wheat and barley with spelt, likewise pulses with legumes and currents with fruit.

$$\text{مَصْرِفُهَا الْفَقِيرُ وَالْمِسْكِينُ} \quad 207$$
$$\text{غَازٍ وَعِتْقُ عَامِلٌ مَدِينُ}$$

207 It is distributed to the poor and the destitute, the
ghazi warrior, in order to set (slaves) free, to the
(zakat) agents and those in debt,

$$\text{مُؤَلَّفُ الْقَلْبِ وَمُحْتَاجٌ غَرِيبْ} \quad 208$$
$$\text{أَحْرَارُ إِسْلَامٍ وَلَمْ يُقْبَلْ مُرِيبْ}$$

208 to those whose hearts may be brought closer (to
Islam), the stranger in need, that is as long as they
are free, Muslim and there is no doubt as to their
state.

$$\text{زَكَاةُ الْفِطْرِ}$$

ZAKAT AL-FITR

$$\text{زَكَاةُ الْفِطْرِ صَاعُ وَتَجِبْ} \quad 209$$
$$\text{عَنْ مُسْلِمٍ وَمَنْ بِرِزْقِهِ طُلِبْ}$$

209 Section: the *zakat al-fitr* is (paid with) a *sa'*, and it is
obligatory on every Muslim and anyone else for
whose upkeep he is responsible -

مِنْ مُسْلِمٍ بِجُلِّ عَيْشِ الْقَوْمِ

لِتُغْنِ حُرّاً مُسْلِماً فِي الْيَوْمِ

210 if they are Muslim, (that is a *sa'*) of the most widely
used foodstuffs of the people – (enough) to feed a
free Muslim for a day.

كِتَابُ الصِّيَامِ

THE BOOK OF FASTING

صِيَامُ شَهْرِ رَمَضَانَ وَجَبَا   211
فِي رَجَبٍ شَعْبَانَ صَوْمٌ نُدِبَا

211 The fast in the month of Ramadan is obligatory, and it is recommended to fast in (the months of) Rajab and Sha'ban

كَتِسْعِ حِجَّةٍ وَأَحْرَى ٱلْآخِرْ   212
كَذَا ٱلْمُحَرَّمُ وَأَحْرَى ٱلْعَاشِرْ

212 (Fasting is also recommended) during the (first) nine days of Dhul-Hijja, and in particular on the last (of these nine days); likewise (all of) Muharram, and in particular on the tenth, that is 'Ashura.

وَيَثْبُتُ الشَّهْرُ بِرُؤْيَةِ الْهِلَالْ

أَوْ بِثَلَاثِينَ قَبِيلاً فِي كَمَالْ

213 The (beginning of the month) is ascertained by
the sighting of the new moon or the completion
of thirty days of the previous month.

فَرْضُ الصِّيَامِ نِيَّةٌ بِلَيْلِهِ

وَتَرْكُ وَطْءٍ شُرْبِهِ وَأَكْلِهِ

214 The obligations of the fast are: making an intention
in the (first) night, abstaining from intercourse,
drinking and eating,

وَالْقَيْءُ مَعْ إِيصَالِ شَيْءٍ لِلْمَعَدْ

مِنْ أُذُنٍ أَوْ عَيْنٍ أَوْ أَنْفٍ وَرَدْ

215 not (deliberately) vomiting and ensuring that
nothing reaches the stomach entering via the ear,
nose, or eye.

وَقْتَ طُلُوعِ فَجْرِهِ إِلَى الْغُرُوبْ

وَالْعَقْلُ فِي أَوَّلِهِ شَرْطُ الْوُجُوبْ

216 The time (of the fast) is from the appearance
of dawn to sunset. Being of sane mind at the
beginning (of the fast) is a condition for its being
obligatory.

وَلْيَقْضِ فَاقِدُهُ وَالْحَيْضُ مَنَعْ   217

صَوْماً وَتَقْضِي الْفَرْضَ إِنْ بِهِ ارْتَفَعْ

217 Any person deprived of this (sanity) must be made up; menstruation prevents fasting, and the woman must make up the obligatory (fast) when it stops.

وَيُكْرَهُ اللَّمْسُ وَفِكْرٌ سَلِمَا   218

دَأْباً مِنَ الْمَذْي وَإِلاَّ حَرُمَا

218 It is makruh to touch (a woman) or allow thoughts (of a sexual nature) – that is, as long as one remains free (of any emission) of pre-seminal fluid; otherwise such (things) are forbidden.

وَكِرِهُوا ذَوْقَ كَقِمْدِرٍ وَهَذَرْ   219

غَالِبُ قَيْءٍ وَذُبَابٍ مُغْتَفَرْ

219 They considered it makruh to taste (something) like (food from) a cooking pot and (to engage in) idle talk; being overcome by vomiting or (swallowing) a fly may be overlooked,

220 غُبَارُ صَانِعٍ وَطُرْقٍ وَسِوَاكْ

يَابِسٍ إِصْبَاحُ جَنَابَةٍ كَذَاكْ

220 as can the dust from (the work of) craftsmen and
from streets, or (the use of) a dry *miswak*; and
likewise, if one awakes in a state of *janaba*.

221 وَنِيَّةٌ تَكْفِي لِمَا تَتَابُعُهْ

يَجِبُ إِلَّا إِنْ نَفَاهُ مَانِعُهْ

221 Making the intention just once is enough for the
obligation (to fast) consecutive (days) except if
interrupted by something which prevents this
(fasting consecutively).

222 نُدِبَ تَعْجِيلٌ لِفِطْرٍ رَفَعَهْ

كَذَاكَ تَأْخِيرُ سُحُورٍ تِبَعَهْ

222 It is recommended to be quick in making the iftar
after the fast, and likewise to delay the suhur
(pre-dawn meal) prior to the fast.

$$\text{مَنْ أَفْطَرَ الْفَرْضَ قَضَاهُ وَلْيَزِدْ} \quad 223$$
$$\text{كَفَّارَةً فِي رَمَضَانَ إِنْ عَمَدْ}$$

223 Whoever breaks an obligatory fast must make it
up and, in addition, pay *kaffara* in Ramadan, if
done deliberately

$$\text{لِأَكْلٍ أَوْ شُرْبٍ فَمٍ أَوْ لِلْمَنِي} \quad 224$$
$$\text{وَلَوْ بِفِكْرٍ أَوْ لِرَفْضٍ مَا بُنِي}$$

224 by eating, drinking or having an emission of
sperm – even if this was (only) as a result of
thoughts (of a sexual nature), or by abandoning
the (intention) upon which the (fast) is based -

$$\text{بِلَا تَأَوُّلٍ قَرِيبٍ وَيُبَاحْ} \quad 225$$
$$\text{لِضُرٍّ أَوْ سَفَرِ قَصْرٍ أَيْ مُبَاحْ}$$

225 without a plausible interpretation; and it is licit (to
break it) if it harms (one's health), or when on a
journey – for a licit purpose – during which one
would shorten the salat.

$$\text{وَعَمْدُهُ فِي النَّفْلِ دُونَ ضُرٍّ} \quad 226$$

$$\text{مُحَرَّمٌ وَلْيَقْضِ لَا فِي الْغَيْـرِ}$$

226 It is prohibited to break a *nafila* fast deliberately
without illness. (If it is broken, however), one must
make it up; but not on account of something else
(i.e. for forgetfulness).

$$\text{وَكَفِّرَنْ بِصَوْمِ شَهْرَيْنِ وِلَا} \quad 227$$

$$\text{أَوْ عِتْقِ مَمْلُوكٍ بِالْإِسْلَامِ حَلَا}$$

227 And *kaffara* is paid by fasting two consecutive
months or freeing a Muslim slave.

$$\text{وَفَضَّلُوا إِطْعَامَ سِتِّينَ فَقِيرْ} \quad 228$$

$$\text{مُدًّا لِمِسْكِينٍ مِنَ الْعَيْشِ الْكَثِيرْ}$$

228 (The fuqaha) have preferred that one feed sixty
poor people, (that is) a *mudd* of the most widely
used food to each destitute person.

كِتَابُ الْحَجِّ

THE BOOK OF HAJJ

اَلْحَجُّ فَرْضٌ مَرَّةً فِي ٱلْعُمْرِ ٢٢٩
أَرْكَانُهُ إِنْ تُرِكَتْ لَمْ تُجْبَرِ

229 The hajj is a *fard* obligation once in a lifetime; if
any of its pillars are left out, it cannot be made
good. (These pillars are:)

اَلْإِحْرَامُ وَالسَّعْيُ وُقُوفُ عَرَفَةْ ٢٣٠
لَيْلَةَ الْأَضْحَى وَالطَّوَافُ رَدِفَةْ

230 entering *ihram*, the *sa'y* between Safa and Marwa,
standing on 'Arafa the night before the Day of
Sacrifice followed by the *tawaf*.

وَالْوَاجِبَاتُ غَيْرُ الْأَرْكَانِ بِدَمْ ٢٣١
قَدْ جُبِرَتْ مِنْهَا طَوَافُ مَنْ قَدِمْ

231 The obligations other than the pillars are
made good by a sacrifice – among them the
tawaf made on arrival,

وَوَصْلُهُ بِالسَّعْيِ مَشْيٌ فِيهِمَا   ٢٣٢

وَرَكْعَةُ الطَّوَافِ إِنْ تُحَتَّمَا

232 and joining it immediately to the *sa'y*, walking
in both, the two *rak'ats* of the *tawaf* if (the *tawaf*
is of the kind which is) incumbent (i.e. *tawaf al-
qudum* and *al-ifada*),

نُـزُولُ مُزْدَلِفٍ فِي رُجُوعِنَا   ٢٣٣

مَبِيتُ لَيْلَاتٍ ثَلَاثٍ بِـمِنَى

233 staying at Muzdalifa on the return, spending
three nights at Mina (after 'Arafa),

إِحْرَامُ مِيقَاتٍ فَذُو الْحُلَيْفَهْ   ٢٣٤

لِـطَيْبَ لِلشَّامِ وَمِصْرَ الْجُحْفَةْ

234 entering the *ihram* via the appointed places at
Dhu'l-Hulayfa for (the people of) Tayb, at al-
Juhfa for Sham (Greater Syria), Egypt (and the
West),

$$\text{قَرْنُ لِنَجْدٍ ذَاتُ عِرْقٍ لِلْعِرَاقْ} \qquad 235$$
$$\text{يَلَمْلَمُ الْيَمَنِ آتِيهَا وِفَاقْ}$$

235 at Qarn for the (highlands of) Najd (of the
Arabian Peninsula), at Dhat al-'Irq for Iraq (Fars
and the east), Yalamyam for the Yemen (and
India) and whoever arrives via these (miqat, even
if not from these regions) should do the same (as
those of these regions),

$$\text{تَجَرُّدٌ مِنَ الْمَخِيطِ تَلْبِيَةْ} \qquad 236$$
$$\text{وَالْحَلْقُ مَعْ رَمْيِ الْجِمَارِ تَوْفِيَةْ}$$

236 not wearing anything sewn, declaring *labbayk,
Allahumma labayk* ..., shaving (the head) and
stoning (the shaytans).

$$\text{وَإِنْ تُرِدْ تَرْتِيبَ حَجِّكَ اسْمَعَا} \qquad 237$$
$$\text{بَيَانَهُ وَالذِّهْنَ مِنْكَ اسْتَجْمِعَا}$$

237 And if you wish (to adhere to) the order (of the
acts) of your hajj, then listen to an explanation (of
it) and concentrate your thoughts:

$$\text{إِنْ جِئْتَ رَابِغاً تَنَظَّفْ وَاغْتَسِلْ} \qquad 238$$
$$\text{كَـــوَاجِبٍ وَبِالشُّرُوعِ يَتَّصِلْ}$$

238 if you arrive at (the village called) Rabigh (on the
   east coast of the Red Sea), then clean yourself
   (by shaving the pubes, plucking the armpits and
   trimming the moustache and nails) and make a
   ghusl like the obligatory (one before jumu'a) just
   before beginning (the *ihram*);

$$\text{وَالْبَسْ رِداً وَأُزْرَةً نَعْلَيْنِ} \qquad 239$$
$$\text{وَاسْتَصْحِبِ الْهَدْيَ وَرَكْـــعَتَيْنِ}$$

239 wear (two pieces of seamless cloth), one about
   the torso and one about the waist and a pair of
   sandals, accompany the sacrificial animal and
   make two *rak'ats*

$$\text{بِالْـكَافِرُونَ ثُمَّ الْإِخْلاصُ هُمَا} \qquad 240$$
$$\text{فَإِنْ رَكِـــبْتَ أَوْ مَشَيْتَ أَحْرِمَا}$$

240 reciting (surat) al-Kafirun – The Rejectors and
   then al-Ikhlas – Sincerity; enter into the *ihram*
   whether you are mounted or walking,

بِنِيَّةٍ تَصْحَبُ قَوْلاً أَوْ عَمَلْ 241

كَـمَشْيٍ أَوْ تَلْبِيَةٍ مِمَّا اتَّصَلْ

241 with the intention, accompanied by the words
associated with it – namely the *talbiya* and the
takbir, or the action (associated with it) – like
(setting out to) walk (towards the places of the
rites) immediately before the (entering the)
ihram;

وَجَدِّدَنْهَا كُلَّمَا تَجَدَّدَتْ 242

حَالٌ وَإِنْ صَلَّيْتَ ثُمَّ إِنْ دَنَتْ

242 and this (*talbiya*) is to be repeated every time
there is a change of state (like standing, sitting or
mounting) or after the salat. When you near

مَكَّةُ فَاغْتَسِلْ بِذِي طُوىً بِلَا 243

دَلْكٍ وَمِنْ كُدَا الثَّنِيَّةِ ادْخُلَا

243 Makka, make a ghusl at Dhu Tuwa without
rubbing (excessively lest one remove some hair)
and enter by (the narrow pass between the two
mountains called) Kuda ath-Thaniya.

إِذَا وَصَلْتَ لِلـبُيُوتِ فَاتْرُكَا 244
تَلْبِيَةً وَكُلَّ شُغْلٍ وَاسْلُكَا

244 When you reach the houses (of Makka) then leave off the invocation of the *talbiya* and all other activity, and go

لِلْبَيْتِ مِنْ بَابِ السَّلَامِ وَاسْتَلِمْ 245
الْحَجَرَ الْأَسْوَدَ كَـــبِّرْ وَأَتِمُّ

245 to the House from the Gate of Peace, kiss the Black Stone, say Allahu akbar and perform

سَبْعَةَ أَشْوَاطٍ بِهِ وَقَدْ يَسَرْ 246
وَكَـــبِّرَنْ مُقَبِّلاً ذَاكَ الْحَجَرْ

246 seven tawafs of the House – with the House on your left, and say Allahu akbar when kissing that stone

مَتَى تُحَاذِيهِ كَـذَا الْيَمَانِي 247
لَـكِنَّ ذَا بِالـيَدِ خُذْ بَـيَانِي

247 whenever passing by it; likewise the Yemeni corner (before it) – however, (greet) this (by touching it) with your hand (and then place it on your mouth), and accept this explanation!

٢٤٨   إِنْ لَمْ تَصِلْ لِلْحَجَرِ الْمَسَّ بِالْيَدِ
وَضَعْ عَلَى الْفَمِ وَكَـــبِّرْ تَقْتَدِ

248 If you do not reach the Black Stone (on the second
tawaf), then touch it with one's hand, place it
on your mouth and say Allahu akbar, thereby
following (the sunna).

٢٤٩   وَارْمُلْ ثَلَاثاً وَامْشِ بَعْدُ أَرْبَعَا
خَلْفَ الْمَقَامِ رَكْـــعَتَيْنِ أَوْقِعَا

249 Walk briskly the (first) three (tawafs) and then walk
the last four (at a normal pace). Then perform
two *rak'ats* behind the Station (of Ibrahim).

٢٥٠   وَادْعُ بِمَا شِئْتَ لَدَى الْمُلْتَزِمِ
وَالْحَجَرَ الْأَسْوَدَ بَعْدُ اسْتَلِمِ

250 Make (as many) du'as as you wish at (the space in
the wall of the Ka'ba known as) al-Multazim and
then kiss the Black Stone.

$$\text{وَاخْرُجْ إِلَى الصَّفَا وَقِفْ مُسْتَقْبِلَا} \quad 251$$
$$\text{عَلَيْهِ ثُمَّ كَـبِّرَنْ وَهَلِّلَا}$$

251 Then go out to Safa and stand facing the
(Ka'ba), exclaim Allahu akbar and (the words
of) the *labbayk*.

$$\text{وَاسْعَ لِـمَرْوَةٍ فَقِفْ مِثْلَ الصَّفَا} \quad 252$$
$$\text{وَخُبَّ فِي بَطْنِ الْمَسِيلِ ذَا اقْتِفَا}$$

252 Then make the *sa'y* to Marwa and stand (there)
like at Safa and make great haste – for this
is following (the sunna) – in Batn al-Maseel
(between the two green markers),

$$\text{أَرْبَعَ وَقْفَاتٍ بِكُلٍّ مِنْهُمَا} \quad 253$$
$$\text{تَقِفُ وَالْأَشْوَاطَ سَبْعاً تَـمِّمَا}$$

253 standing four times at each of the two and
complete the seven going to and fro.

$$\text{وَادْعُ بِمَا شِئْتَ بِسَعْيٍ وَطَوَافْ} \quad 254$$
$$\text{وَبِالصَّفَا وَمَرْوَةٍ مَعَ اعْتِرَافْ}$$

254 Make du'a as (much as) you wish during the *sa'y*
and *tawaf*, and at Safa and Marwa, in a state of
recognition (of your wrong actions).

$$\text{255} \qquad \text{وَيَجِبُ الطُّهْرَانِ وَالسَّتْرُ عَلَى}$$
$$\text{مَنْ طَافَ نَدْبهَا بِسَعْيٍ يُجْتَلَى}$$

255 It is obligatory for the person doing the *tawaf* to
be free of impurity (both on oneself and one's
clothes), to be in a state of ritual purity and to
cover (one's private parts); and it is recommended
for the *sa'y* as a particular mark of excellence.

$$\text{256} \qquad \text{وَعُدْ فَلَبِّ لِمُصَلَّى عَرَفَةْ}$$
$$\text{وَخُطْبَةُ السَّابِعِ تَأْتِي لِلصِّفَةْ}$$

256 Resume the saying of the *talbiya* until (reaching)
the musalla of 'Arafa; and (attend) the khutba
of the seventh say (of Dhu'l-Hijja) – this is a
description (of what is correct)!

$$\text{257} \qquad \text{وَثَامِنَ الشَّهْرِ انْخُرْجَنَّ لِمِنَى}$$
$$\text{بِعَرَفَاتٍ تَاسِعاً نُزُولُنَا}$$

257 On the eighth of the month go out to Mina and
dismount at 'Arafa on the ninth.

258 وَاغْتَسِلَنْ قُرْبَ الزَّوَالِ وَاحْضُرَا
الْخُطْبَتَيْنِ وَاجْمَعَنْ وَقَصِّرَا

258 Take a ghusl just after the sun has past its zenith,
attend the two khutbas, and join and shorten the
salats

259 ظُهْرَيْكَ ثُمَّ الْجَبَلَ اصْعَدْ رَاكِبًا
عَلَى وُضُوءٍ ثُمَّ كُنْ مُوَاظِبَا

259 of dhuhr and 'asr. Then ascend the mount,
(preferably) mounted (on one's riding beast), and
in a state of wudu'. Persevere in

260 عَلَى الدُّعَا مُهَلِّلاً مُبْتَهِلَا
مُصَلِّيًا عَلَى النَّبِي مُسْتَقْبِلَا

260 making du'a, saying *la ilaha illallah*, humbly
supplicating, sending blessings on the Prophet
while facing the qibla.

261 هُنَيْهَةً بَعْدَ غُرُوبِهَا تَقِفْ
وَانْفِرْ لِمُزْدَلِفَةٍ وَتَنْصَرِفْ

261 Stand a little while after the sunset, then hasten to
Muzdalifa making your way

$$في الْمَأْزِمَيْنِ الْعَلَمَيْنِ نَكِّبِ \qquad 262$$
$$وَقَصِّرْ بِهَا وَاجْمَعْ عِشاً لِمَغْرِبِ$$

262 between the two mountains (called the)
Ma'zamayn avoiding (other than this way), and
then shorten and join maghrib and 'isha in
(Muzdalifa).

$$وَاحْطُطْ وَبِتْ بِهَا وَأَحْيِ لَيْلَتَكْ \qquad 263$$
$$وَصَلِّ صُبْحَكَ وَغَلِّسْ رِحْلَتَكْ$$

263 Dismount (with your saddles and belongings) and
spend the night there (in Muzdalifa) filling it with
dhikr and salat. Pray your subh salat and then
move off as light starts to break.

$$قِفْ وَادْعُ بِالْمَشْعَرِ لِلْأَسْفَارِ \qquad 264$$
$$وَأَسْرِعَنْ فِي بَطْنِ وَادِي النَّارِ$$

264 Stand and make du'a at the Mash'ar (at Muzdalifa)
before sunrise and make haste at the bottom of
Wadi an-Nar (also known as Batn al-Muhassir).

265 وَسِرْ كَـــمَا تَكُونُ لِلْعَقَبَة
فَارْمِ لَدَيْهَا بِحِجَارٍ سَبْعَة

265 Go as you are (either mounted or walking) to the
(*jamrat*) al-'Aqaba and throw the seven pebbles
there

266 مِنْ أَسْفَلٍ تُسَاقُ مِنْ مُزْدَلِفَة
كَالْفُولِ وَانْحَرْ هَدْياً إِنْ بِعَرَفَة

266 from below, having brought them along with you
from Muzdalifa, (the pebbles being) about the
size of beans. Sacrifice the *hady* if at 'Arafa

267 أَوْقَفْتَهُ وَاحْلِقْ وَسِرْ لِلْبَيْتِ
فَطُفْ وَصَلِّ مِثْلَ ذَاكَ النَّعْتِ

267 you had stopped, then shave, continue to the
House and perform the *tawaf* (*al-ifada*), praying
(two *rak'ats*) as described (before).

268 وَارْجِعْ فَصَلِّ الظُّهْرَ فِي مِنًى وَبِتْ
إِثْرَ زَوَالِ غَدِهِ أَرْمِ لَا تُفِتْ

268 Then return and pray dhuhr at Mina (the day
of the 'Eid) and remain (three) nights (if possible).
Immediately after the sun passes its zenith, you
must go and stone

$$\text{ثَلَاثَ جَمْرَاتٍ بِسَبْعِ حَصَيَاتْ} \quad 269$$

$$\text{لِكُلِّ جَمْرَةٍ وَقْفٌ لِلدَّعَوَاتْ}$$

269 the three jamras, each with seven pebbles and
stand – making du'a –

$$\text{طَوِيلاً إِثْرَ الْأَوَّلَيْنِ أَخِّرَا} \quad 270$$

$$\text{عَقَبَةً وَكُلَّ رَمْيٍ كَــبِّرَا}$$

270 for a considerable time after the first two; then
finish with the (jamrat) al-'Aqaba (that is, after the
one next to the mosque of Mina and the middle
jamra); and for each stoning say Allahu akbar.

$$\text{وَافْعَلْ كَذَاكَ ثَالِثَ النَّحْرِ وَزِدْ} \quad 271$$

$$\text{إِنْ شِئْتَ رَابِعاً وَتَمَّ مَا قُصِدْ}$$

271 Do likewise on the third day and add if you wish
a fourth (day), and what was intended is now
completed.

$$\text{وَمَنَعَ الْإِحْرَامُ صَيْدَ الْبَرِّ} \quad 272$$

$$\text{فِي قَتْلِهِ الْجَزَاءُ لَا كَالْفَأْرِ}$$

272 The (state of) ihram prohibits hunting on land, and
compensation has to be made if (game is) killed,
but not (creatures) like mice (or rats),

273 وَعَقْرَبٍ مَعَ الْحِدَا كَلْبٍ عَقُورْ
وَحَيَّةٍ مَعَ الْغُرَابِ إذْ يَجُورْ

273 scorpions, vultures (or kites), wild beasts (like lions, tigers or wolves), snakes, or crows (and ravens) if (any of these) are causing harm.

274 وَمَنَعَ الْمَخِيطِ بِالْعُضْوِ وَلَوْ
بِنَسْجٍ أَوْ عَقْدٍ نِكَاتَمِ حَكُوا

274 It also proscribes the wearing of clothing which are (fashioned and) sewn to (cover the form of the limbs), or something woven which is fixed with a button or clasp, or (the wearing of) a ring;

275 وَالسَّتْرُ لِلْوَجْهِ أَوِ الرَّأْسِ بِمَا
يُعَدُّ سَاتِراً وَلَكِنْ إِنَّمَا

275 or covering the face or head with anything which may be (properly) termed a covering; but it only

تَمْنَعُ الأُنْثَى لُبْسَ قُفَّازٍ كَذَا   276
سَتْـرُ لِوَجْهِ لَا لِسَتْرٍ أُخِذَا

276 prohibits a woman from wearing gloves (*quffaz*)
 – in addition to covering her face, but not if she
 takes a veil (to protect her from the importune
 gazes of men);

وَمَنَعَ الطِّيبَ وَدُهْناً وَضَرَرْ   277
قَمْلٍ وَإِلْقَا وَسِخٍ ظُفْرٍ شَعَرْ

277 prohibited also is (the wearing of) perfume and
 oil (in the hair or beard), killing (and removing)
 lice, or removing dirt, nails or hair –

وَيَفْتَدِي لِفِعْلِ بَعْضٍ مَا ذُكِرْ   278
مِنَ الْمُخِيطِ لِهُنَا وَإِنْ عُذِرْ

278 and compensation (*fidya*) must be paid if any of
 the above mentioned occurs, from sewed clothing
 right up to here, even if he has a valid excuse;

$$\text{وَمَنَعَ النِّسَا وَأَفْسَدَ الْجِمَاعْ} \qquad 279$$
$$\text{إِلَى الْإِفَاضَةِ يُـبَقَّى الِامْتِنَاعْ}$$

279 also prohibited is (having any sexual contact with) women, (including marriage), and intercourse invalidates (the hajj), and this prohibition lasts until the (*tawaf*) *al-ifada*;

$$\text{كَالصَّيْدِ ثُمَّ بَاقِي مَا قَدْ مُنِعَا} \qquad 280$$
$$\text{بِالْجَمْرَةِ الْأُولَى يَحِلُّ فَاسْمَعَا}$$

280 as for hunting (prohibited), then the other things which are prohibited for him, these are rendered halal at the stoning of the *jamrat al-ula* (the first *jamra*) – so heed (these instructions)!

$$\text{وَجَازَ الِاسْتِظْلَالُ بِالْمُرْتَفِعْ} \qquad 281$$
$$\text{لَا فِي الْمَحَامِلَ وَشُقْدُفٍ فَعِ}$$

281 It is permitted to shade oneself with something raised (of a fixed nature, above one's head), but not (by means of the roof of) a litter or a shuqduf sedan – so take note!

$$\text{وَسُنَّةَ الْعُمْرَةِ فَافْعَلْهَا كَـمَا} \quad 282$$

$$\text{حَجَّ وَفِي التَّنْعِيمِ نَدْباً أَحْرِمَا}$$

282 Perform the sunna of the 'umra as the (first part
of the) hajj. It is recommended to put on the *ihram*
at at-Tan'eem.

$$\text{وَإِثْرَ سَعْيِكَ احْلِقَنْ وَقَصِّرَا} \quad 283$$

$$\text{تُحِلُّ مِنْهاَ وَالطَّوَافَ كَـثِّـرَا}$$

283 Immediately following your *sa'y*, shave (your
head) or trim (your hair), leave the state of *ihram*
and perform the *tawaf* frequently

$$\text{مَا دُمْتَ فِي مَكَّةَ وَارْعَ الْحُرْمَةْ} \quad 284$$

$$\text{لِجَانِبِ الْبَيْتِ وَزِدْ فِي الْخِدْمَةْ}$$

284 as long as you are in Makka. Take care to observe
the sanctity (of Makka) as well as the House,
increase your (acts of) service (to Allah ta'ala)

$$\text{وَلَازِمِ الصَّفَّ فَإِنْ عَزَمْتَ} \quad 285$$

$$\text{عَلَى الْخُرُوجِ طُفْ كَمَا عَلِمْتَ}$$

285 and maintain the salat in *jama'a*. When you are
resolved to leave, make the *tawaf* (in the same
manner) as you have learned of above.

زِيَارَةُ سَيِّدِنَا وَمَوْلَانَا
مُحَمَّدِ بْنِ عَبْدِ اللَّهِ رَسُولِ اللَّهِ

VISITING OUR CHIEF AND MASTER, MUHAMMAD IBN 'ABDALLAH, THE MESSENGER OF ALLAH

وَسِرْ لِقَبْرِ الْمُصْطَفَى بِأَدَبٍ ۝ ٢٨٦
وَنِـــيَّةٍ تُجَبْ لِكُلِّ مَطْلَبِ

286 Go to the tomb of Mustafa, the Chosen One, with adab and (a clear) intention and your every request will be answered.

سَلِّمْ عَلَيْهِ ثُمَّ زِدْ لِلصِّدِّيقْ ۝ ٢٨٧
ثُمَّ إِلَى عُمَرَ نِلْتَ التَّوْفِيقْ

287 Greet him, and then go to (Abu Bakr) as-Siddiq, then to 'Umar, and you will have success!

$$\text{وَاعْلَمْ بِأَنَّ ذَا الْمَقَامِ يُسْتَجَابْ}$$

288

$$\text{فِيهِ الدُّعَا فَلَا تَمَلَّ مِنْ طِلَابْ}$$

288 Know that du'as are answered at this station, and
so do not tire from asking.

$$\text{وَسَلْ شَفَاعَةً وَخَتْماً حَسَنَا}$$

289

$$\text{وَعِجِّلِ الْأَوْبَةَ إِذْ نِلْتَ الْمُنَا}$$

289 Ask for intercession and a good seal (on death),
and hurry to return since you have obtained your
desire.

$$\text{وَادْخُلْ ضُحًى وَاصْحَبْ هَدِيَّةَ السُّرُورْ}$$

290

$$\text{إِلَى الْأَقَارِبِ وَمَنْ بِكَ يَدُورْ}$$

290 Make your arrival in the morning and bring
gifts to (gladden the hearts of) relatives and those
living around you.

كِتَابُ مَبَادِئُ التَّصَوُّف
وَهَوَادِي التَّعَرُّف

THE PRINCIPLES OF TASAWWUF
AND THE GUIDES TO
REALISATION

وَتَوْبَةٌ مِنْ كُلِّ ذَنْبٍ يُجْتَرَمْ   291
تَجِبُ فَوْراً مُطْلَقاً وَهِيَ النَّدَمْ

291 It is obligatory to turn in tawba immediately and
absolutely from all wrong action committed, and
this means regret –

بِشَرْطِ الإِقْلَاعِ وَنَفِي الإِصْرَارْ   292
وَلْيَتَلَافَ مُمْكِناً ذَا اسْتِغْفَارْ

292 conditional upon eliminating this (wrong action
from one's behaviour) and not persevering in
it; and one possible way of making redress is
through seeking forgiveness.

$$293 \quad \text{وحَاصِلُ التَّقْوَى اجْتِنَابٌ وَامْتِثَالْ}$$

$$\text{فِي ظَاهِرٍ وَبَاطِنٍ بِذَا تُنَالْ}$$

293 The outcome of taqwa is avoidance (of wrong action) and compliance (with what has been commanded) in the outward and in the inward (with respect to both the 'avoiding' and 'the following'); by that it is obtained!

$$294 \quad \text{فَجَاءَتِ الأَقْسَامُ حَقًّا أَرْبَعَةْ}$$

$$\text{وَهِيَ لِلسَّالِكِ سُبْلُ الْمَنْفَعَةْ}$$

294 and so this amounts to four kinds (of means in all), and for the person travelling on the Path they represent the means and access to benefit.

$$295 \quad \text{يَغُضُّ عَيْنَيْهِ عَنِ الْمَحَارِمْ}$$

$$\text{يَكُفُّ سَمْعَهُ عَنِ الْمَآثِمْ}$$

295 One lowers one's eyes before the haram, and seal off one's hearing from any blameworthy matter,

$$كَغِيبَةٍ نَمِيمَةٍ زُورٍ كَذِبْ$$
$$لِسَانَهُ أَحْرَى بِتَرْكِ مَا جُلِبْ$$

296 as, for example, backbiting, slander, bearing
false witness or lying, and more importantly
one's tongue should avoid saying anything just
mentioned.

$$يَحْفَظُ بَطْنَهُ مِنَ الْحَرَامْ$$
$$يَتْرُكُ مَا شُبِّهَ بِاهْتِمَامْ$$

297 He should guard his belly from what is haram
and be assiduous in avoiding what is doubtful.

$$يَحْفَظُ فَرْجَهُ وَيَتَّقِي الشَّهِيدْ$$
$$فِي الْبَطْشِ وَالسَّعْيِ لَمَمْنُوعٍ يُرِيدْ$$

298 He must protect his private parts, and have fearful
awareness of the One who witnesses (him) when
he takes (something) or strives for something
prohibited which he wants.

$$وَيُوقِفُ الأُمُورَ حَتَّى يَعْلَمَا$$
$$مَا اللهُ فِيهِنَّ بِهِ قَدْ حَكَمَا$$

299 He should desist from matters until he knows
what Allah has ruled for them.

$$\text{يُطَهِّرُ الْقَلْبَ مِنَ الرِّيَاء} \quad 300$$
$$\text{وَحَسَدٍ عُجْبٍ وكُلِّ دَاءٍ}$$

300 He must purify his heart from showing off, from envy, conceit and every (other) sickness.

$$\text{وَاعْلَمْ بِأَنَّ أَصْلَ ذِي الْآفَاتِ} \quad 301$$
$$\text{حُبُّ الرِّيَاسَةِ وَطَرْحُ الْآتِي}$$

301 Know that the root of all blight is love of leadership (rank, praise, honour and ease in this world) and rejection of (the life) to come;

$$\text{رَأْسُ الْخَطَايَا هُوَ حُبُّ الْعَاجِلَةْ} \quad 302$$
$$\text{لَيْسَ الدَّوَا إِلاَّ فِي الاِضْطِرَارِ لَهْ}$$

302 that the chief of all faults is love of this world, and that there is no cure but to be in need of Him.

$$\text{يَصْحَبُ شَيْخاً عَارِفَ الْمَسَالِكْ} \quad 303$$
$$\text{يَقِيهِ فِي طَرِيقِهِ الْمَهَالِكْ}$$

303 He must keep the company of a Shaykh who has knowledge of the ways and who will protect him on his path from dangers;

يُذَكِّرُهُ اللَّهَ إِذَا رَآهُ ٣٠٤

وَيُوصِلُ الْعَبْدَ إِلَى مَوْلَاهُ

304 he reminds him of Allah when he sees him, and he brings the slave to His Lord.

يُحَاسِبُ النَّفْسَ عَلَى الْأَنْفَاسِ ٣٠٥

وَيَزِنُ الْخَاطِرَ بِالْقِسْطَاسِ

305 He takes the self to account for every breath and weighs his thoughts and feelings in the balance

وَيَحْفَظُ الْمَفْرُوضَ رَأْسَ الْمَالِ ٣٠٦

وَالنَّفْلَ رِبْحَهُ بِهِ يُوَالِي

306 He must preserve the *fard* obligation which is his capital, just as the *nafila* acts are his profit, by which he befriends (Allah)

وَيُكْثِرُ الذِّكْرَ بِصَفْوِ لُبِّهِ ٣٠٧

وَالْعَوْنُ فِي جَمِيعِ ذَا بِرَبِّهِ

307 He increases dhikr by means of the purity of his core, and help in all of this is by means of his Lord.

$$\text{يُجَاهِدُ النَّفْسَ لِرَبِّ الْعَالَمِينْ} \quad 308$$
$$\text{وَيَتَخَلَّى بِمَقَامَاتِ الْيَقِينْ}$$

308 He struggles against the self for the sake of the
Lord of the Worlds, and he will be adorned with
the stations of certainty,

$$\text{خَوْفٌ رَجاً شُكْرٌ وَصَبْرٌ تَوْبَةْ} \quad 309$$
$$\text{زُهْدٌ تَوَكُّلٌ رِضاً مَحَبَّةْ}$$

309 fear, hope, gratitude, patience, tawba, doing
without, reliance, contentment and love.

$$\text{يَصْدُقُ شَاهِدَهُ فِي الْمُعَامَلَةْ} \quad 310$$
$$\text{يَرْضَى بِمَا قَدَّرَهُ الْإِلَهُ لَهْ}$$

310 He is true towards the One Who witnesses in his
transactions; and is content with what his Lord
has decreed for him.

$$\text{يَصِيرُ عِنْدَ ذَاكَ عَارِفاً بِهِ} \quad 311$$
$$\text{حُرّاً وَغَيْرُهُ خَلَا مِنْ قَلْبِهِ}$$

311 Then he will become a gnostic of Allah, free, and
other-than-Allah will leave his heart.

$$\text{كَبَّهُ الإِلَهُ وَاصْطَفَاهُ} \qquad 312$$
$$\text{لِحَضْرَةِ الْقُدُّوسِ واجْتَبَاهُ}$$

312 Then Allah will love him, will choose him for the presence of the Sacred and elect him (over others).

$$\text{ذَا الْقَدْرُ نَظْماً لَا يَفِي بِالْغَايَةِ} \qquad 313$$
$$\text{وَفِي الَّذِي ذَكَرْتُهُ كِفَايَةٌ}$$

313 Although these lines do not encompass the full spectrum (of this science), there is enough in what I have mentioned (to set about this path).

$$\text{أَبْيَاتُهُ أَرْبَعَةُ عَشَرَ تَصِلْ} \qquad 314$$
$$\text{مَعَ ثَلَاثِمَائَةٍ عَدُّ الرُّسُلْ}$$

314 It has three hundred and fourteen verses – the number of the Messengers.

$$\text{سَمَّيتُهُ بِالْمُرْشِدِ الْمُعِينِ} \qquad 315$$
$$\text{عَلَى الضَّرُورِي مِنْ عُلُومِ الدِّينِ}$$

315 I called it the *al-Murshid al-Mu'een* – the Concise Guide to the Basics of the Deen.

$$316 \qquad \text{فَأَسْأَلُ النَّفْعَ بِهِ عَلَى الدَّوَامْ}$$

$$\text{مِنْ رَبِّنَا بِجَاهِ سَيِّدِ الْأَنَامْ}$$

316 So I ask our Lord by the rank of the Chief of
Mankind that perpetual benefit come from it

$$317 \qquad \text{قَدِ انْتَهَى وَالْحَمْدُ لِلَّهِ الْعَظِيمْ}$$

$$\text{صَلَّى وَسَلَّمَ عَلَى الْهَادِي الْكَرِيمْ}$$

317 It is concluded, and praise belongs to Allah the
Tremendous, may He bless and grant peace to
the Generously Noble Guide.

www.ingramcontent.com/pod-product-compliance
Lightning Source LLC
Chambersburg PA
CBHW060120050426
42448CB00010B/1955